Flowers

Angie's Patterns - Volume 8

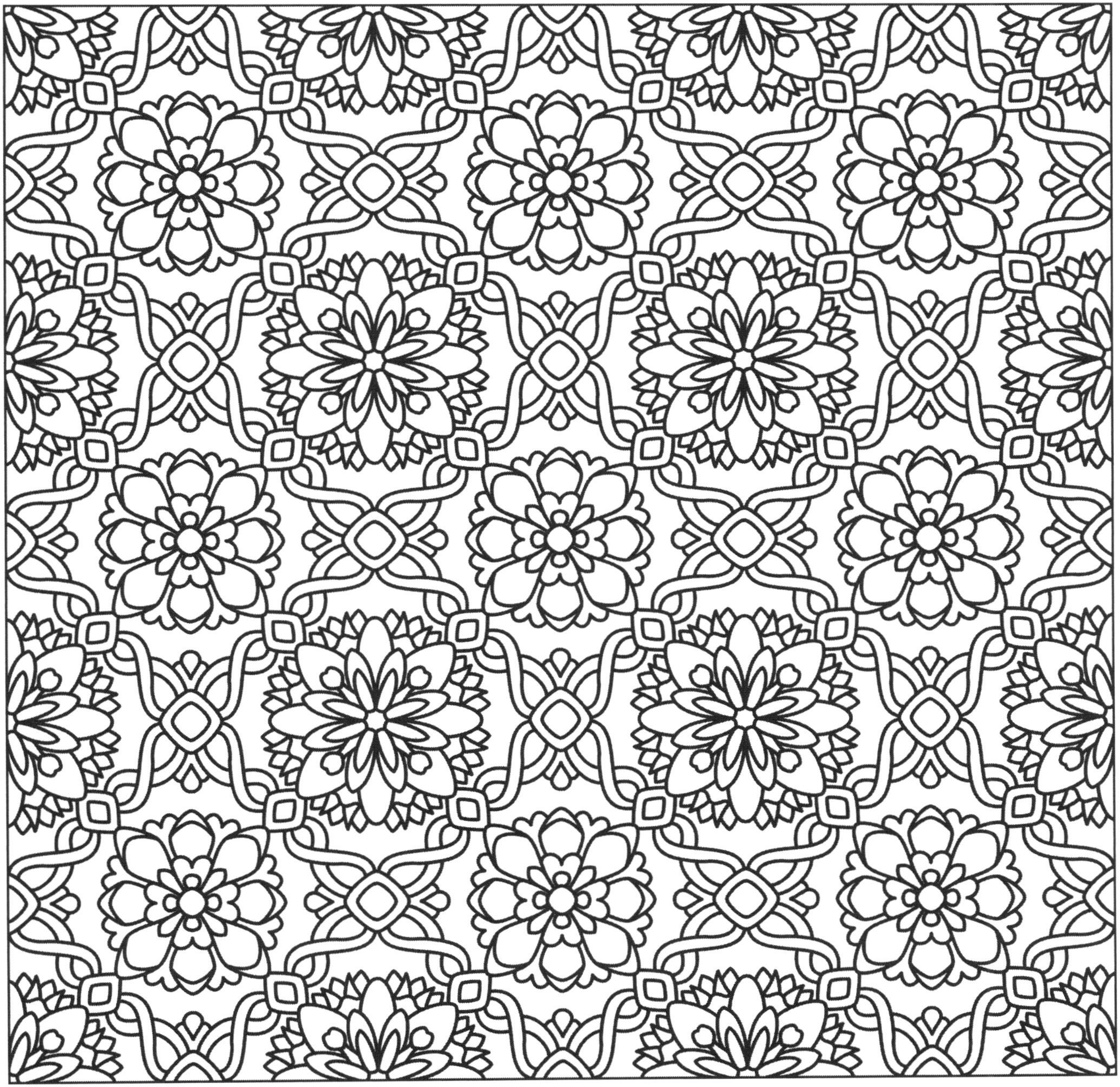

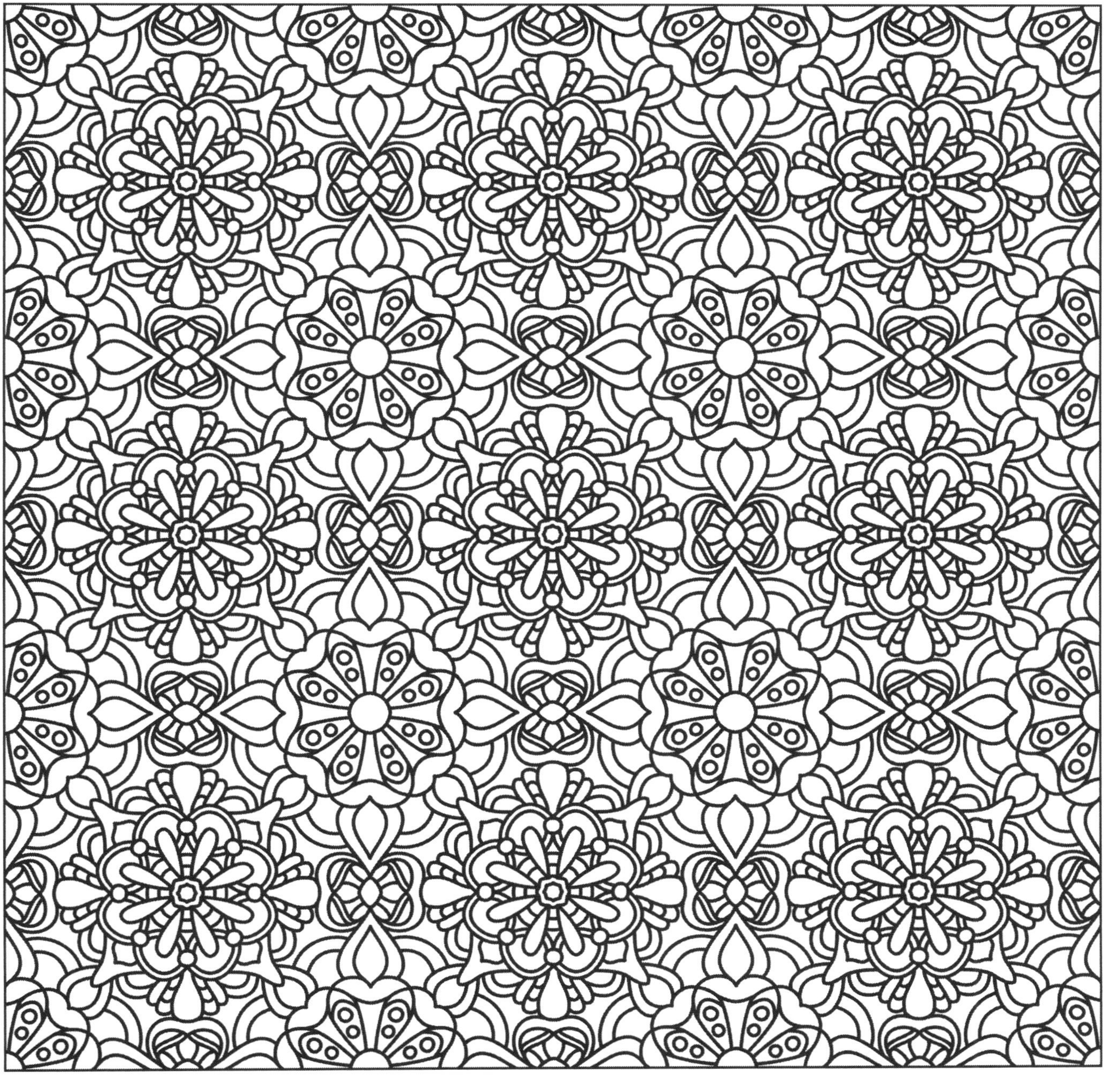

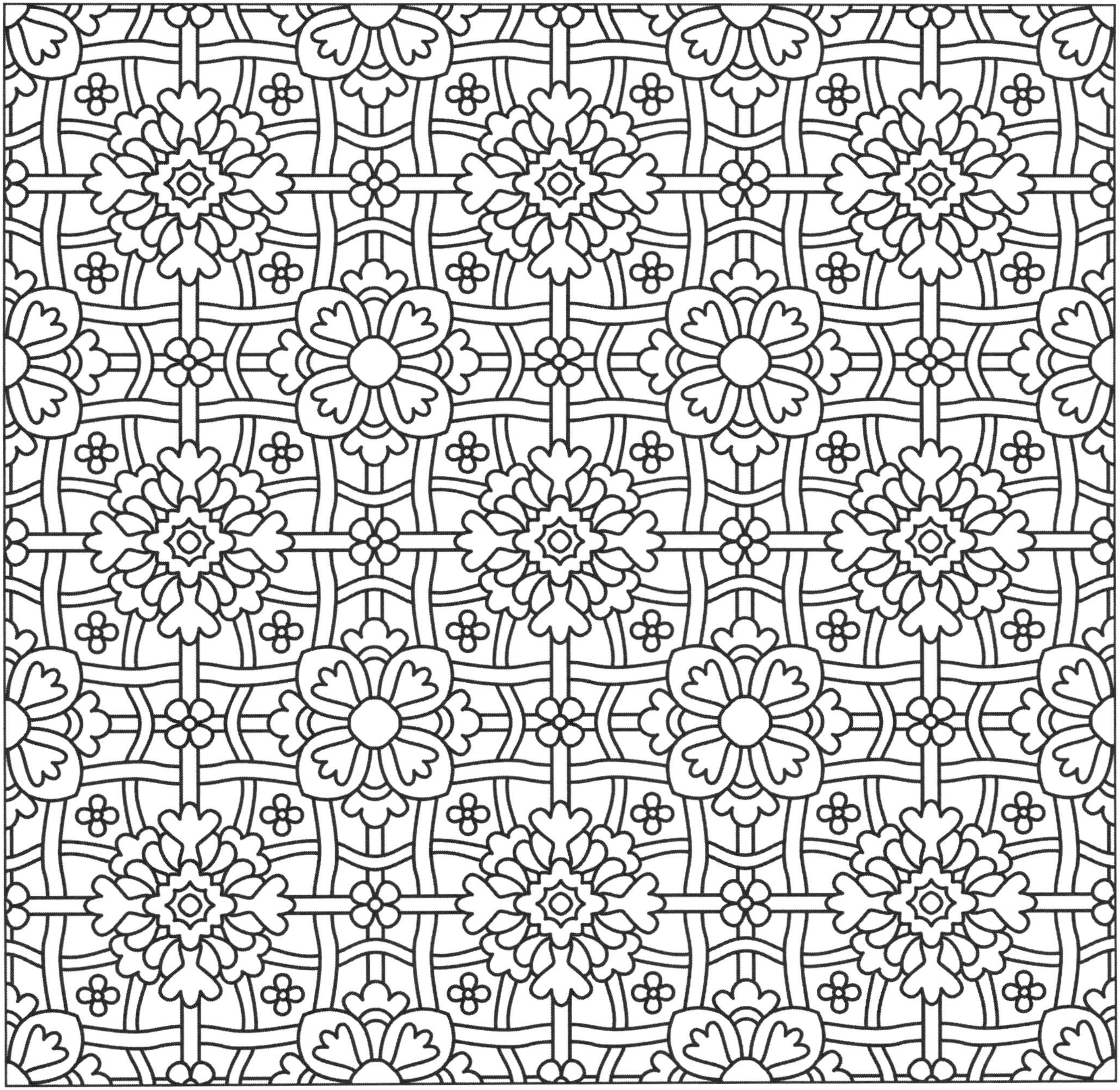

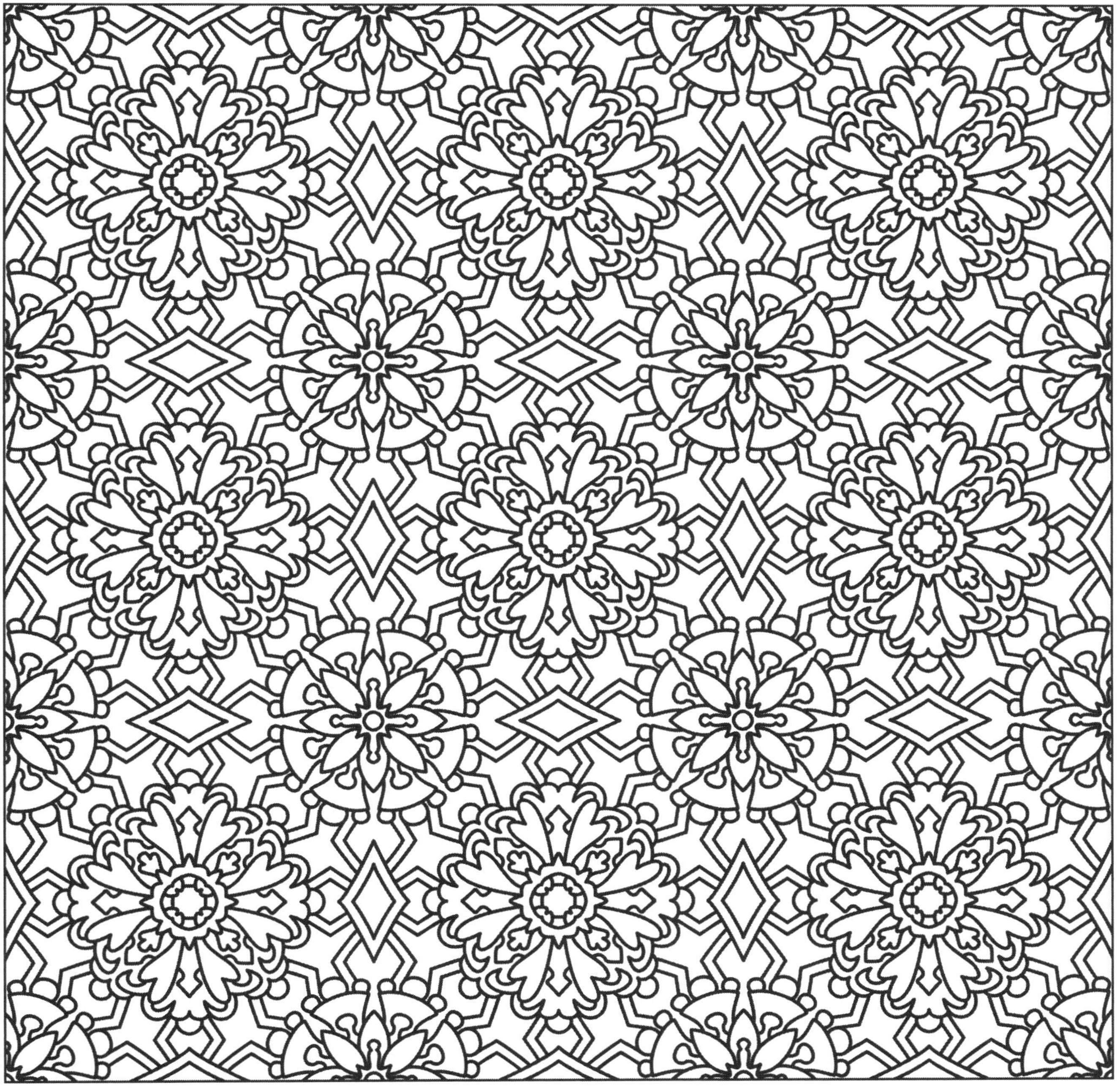

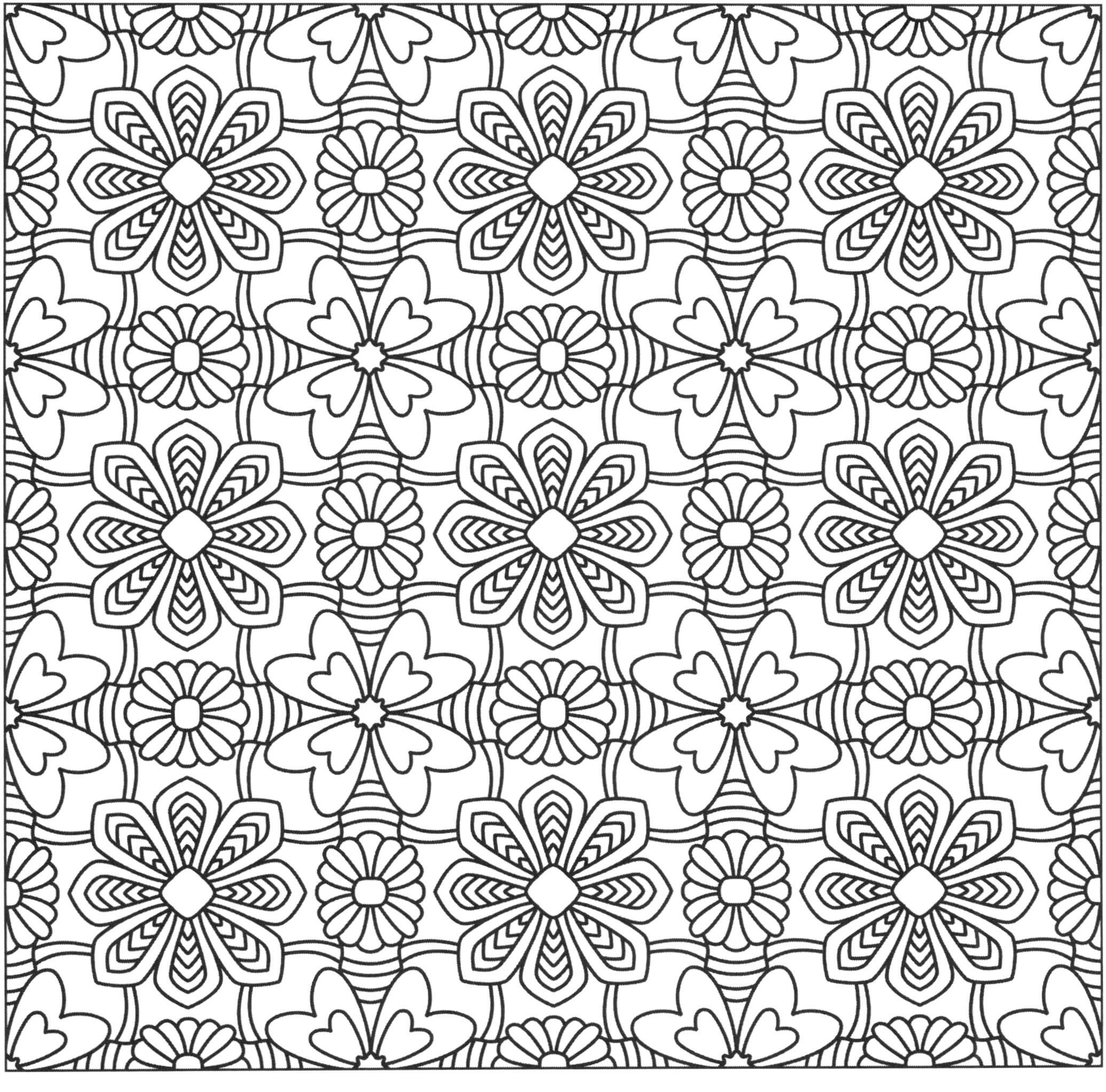

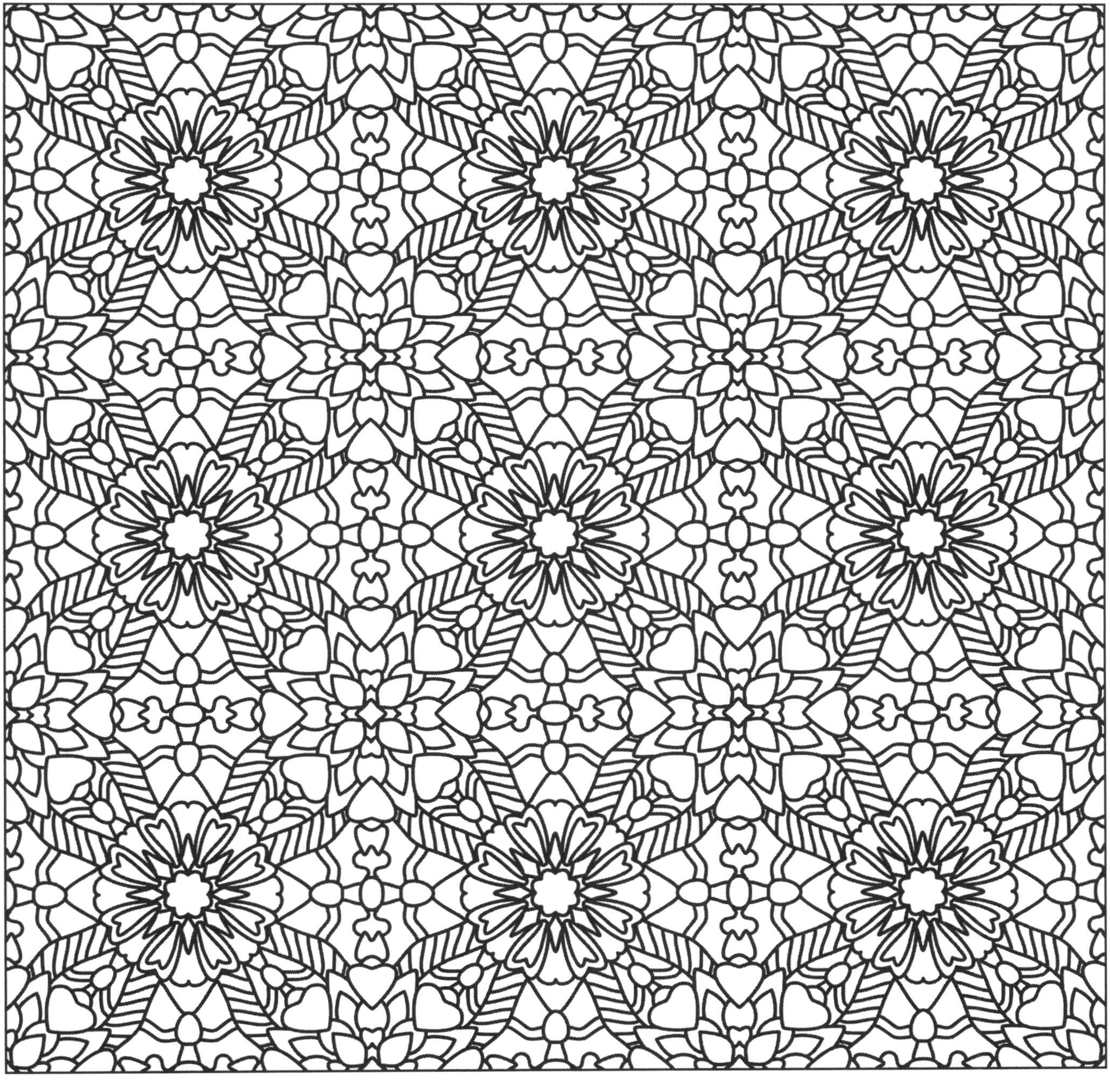

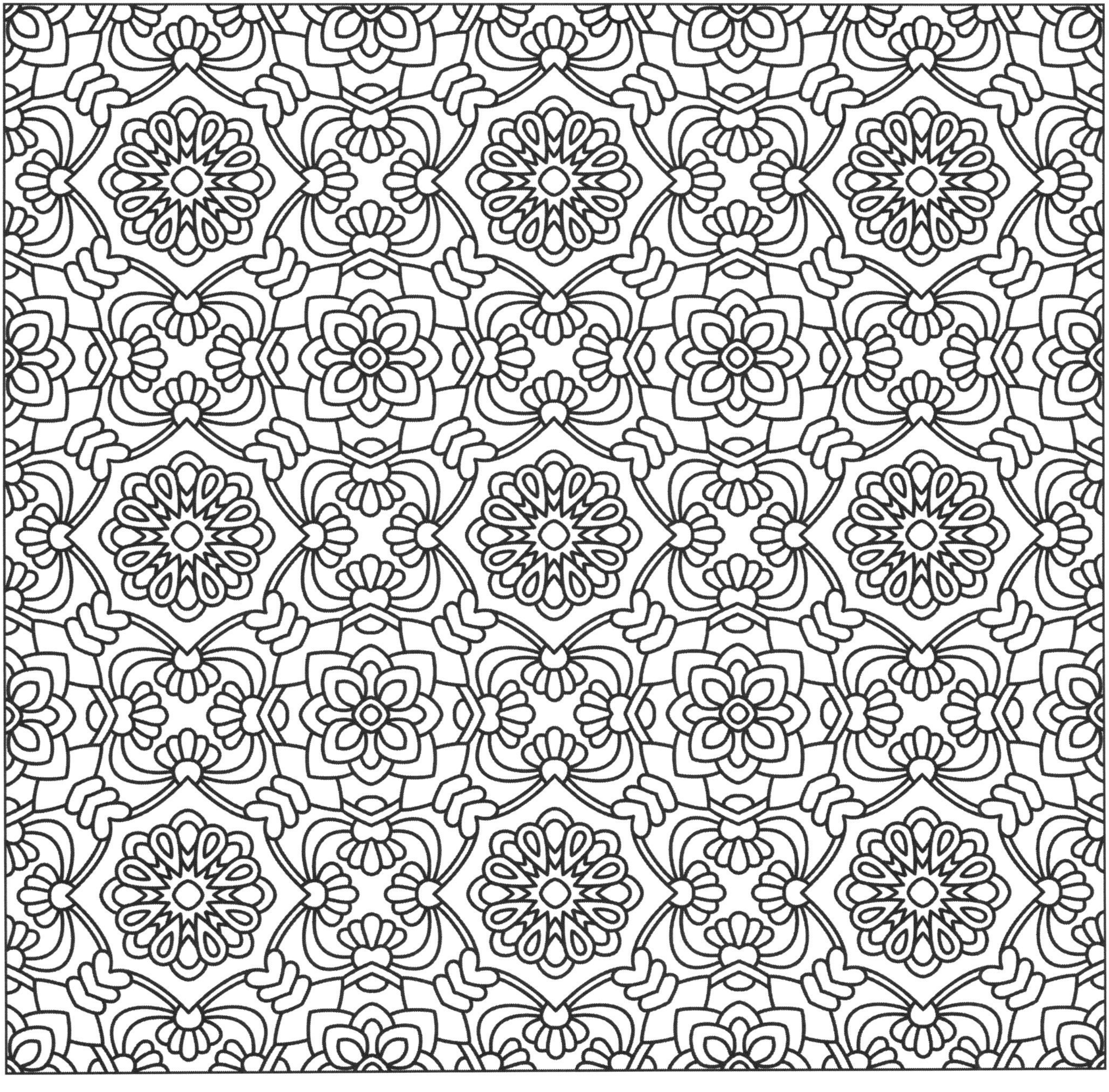

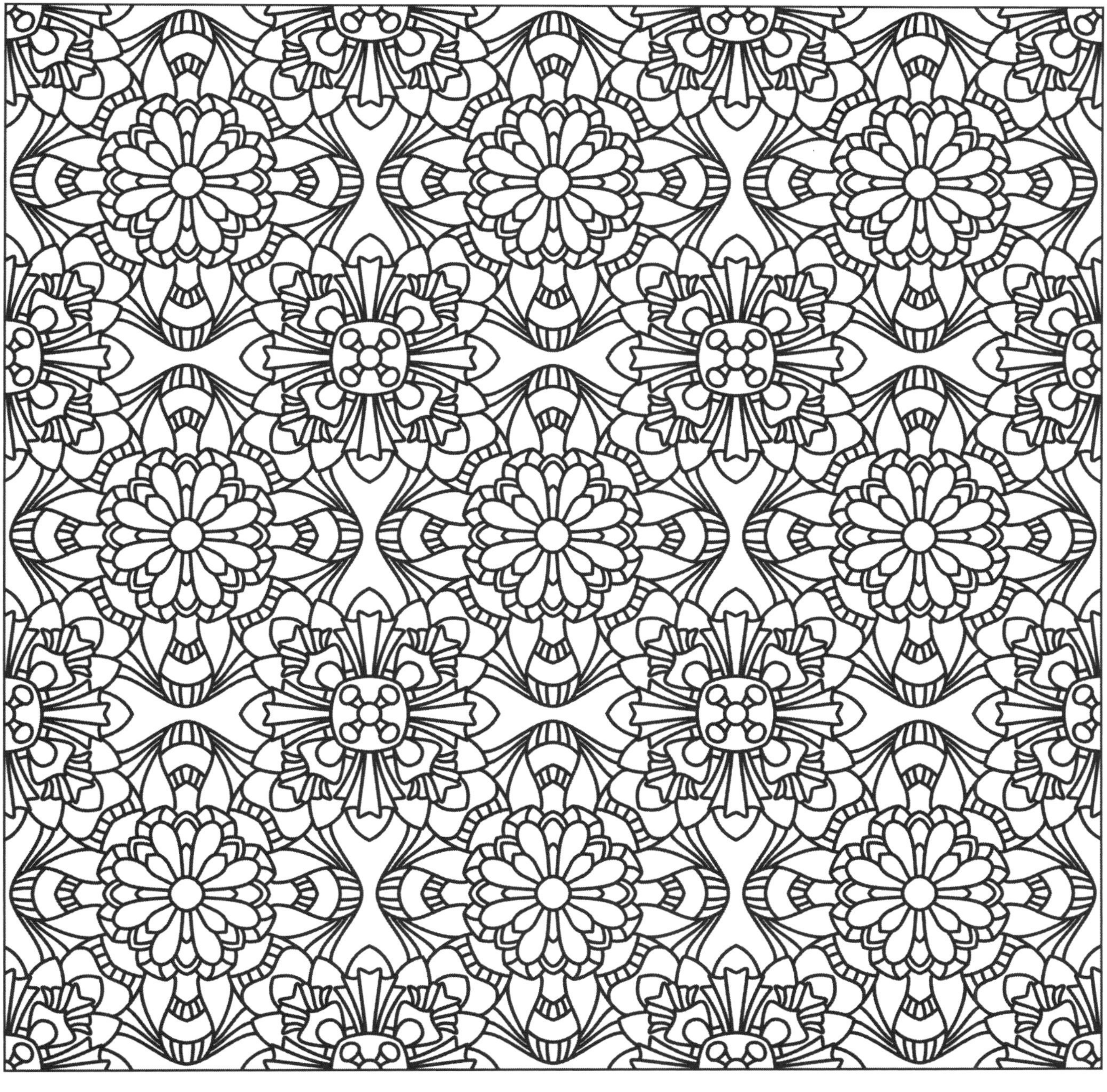

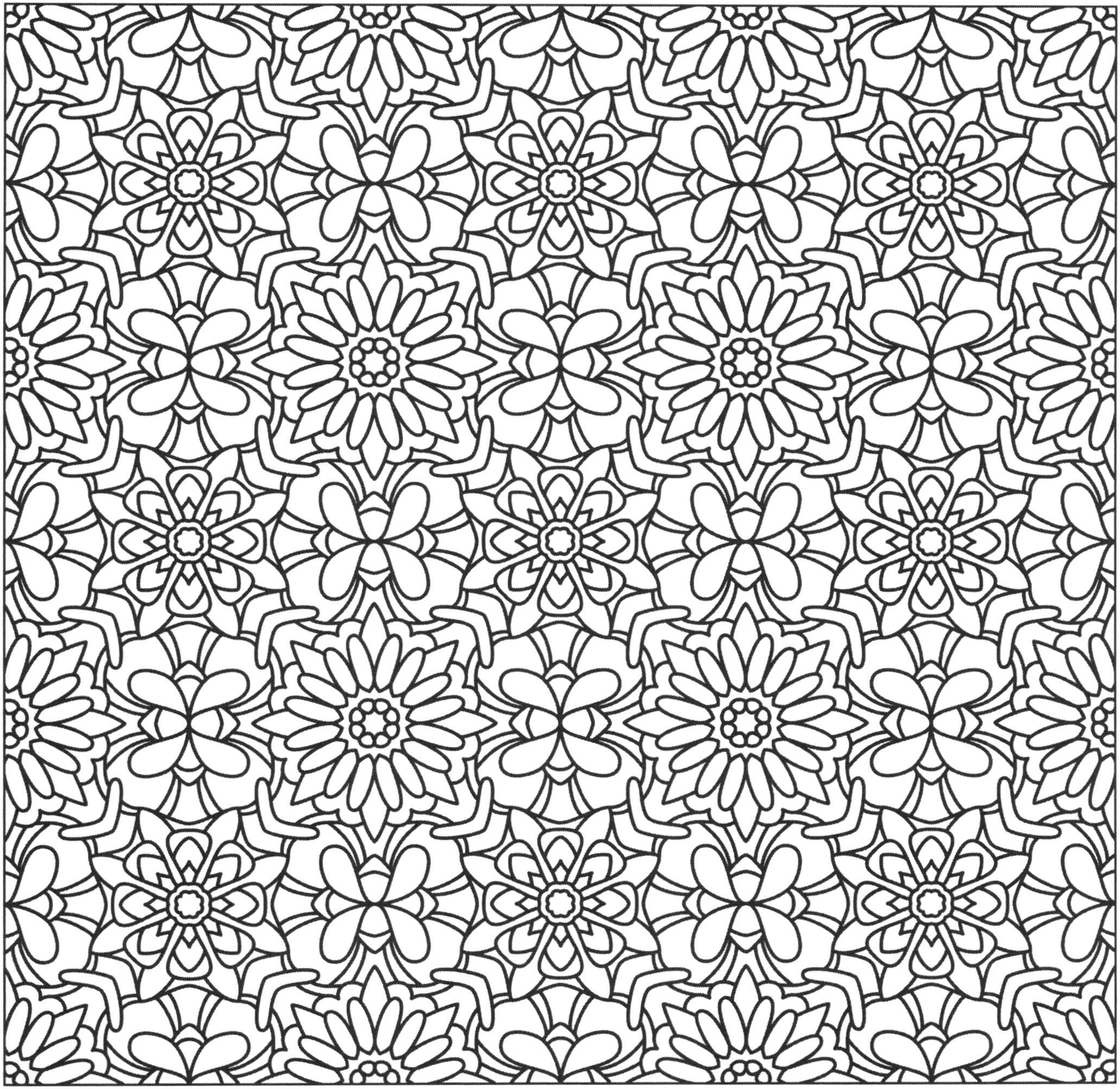

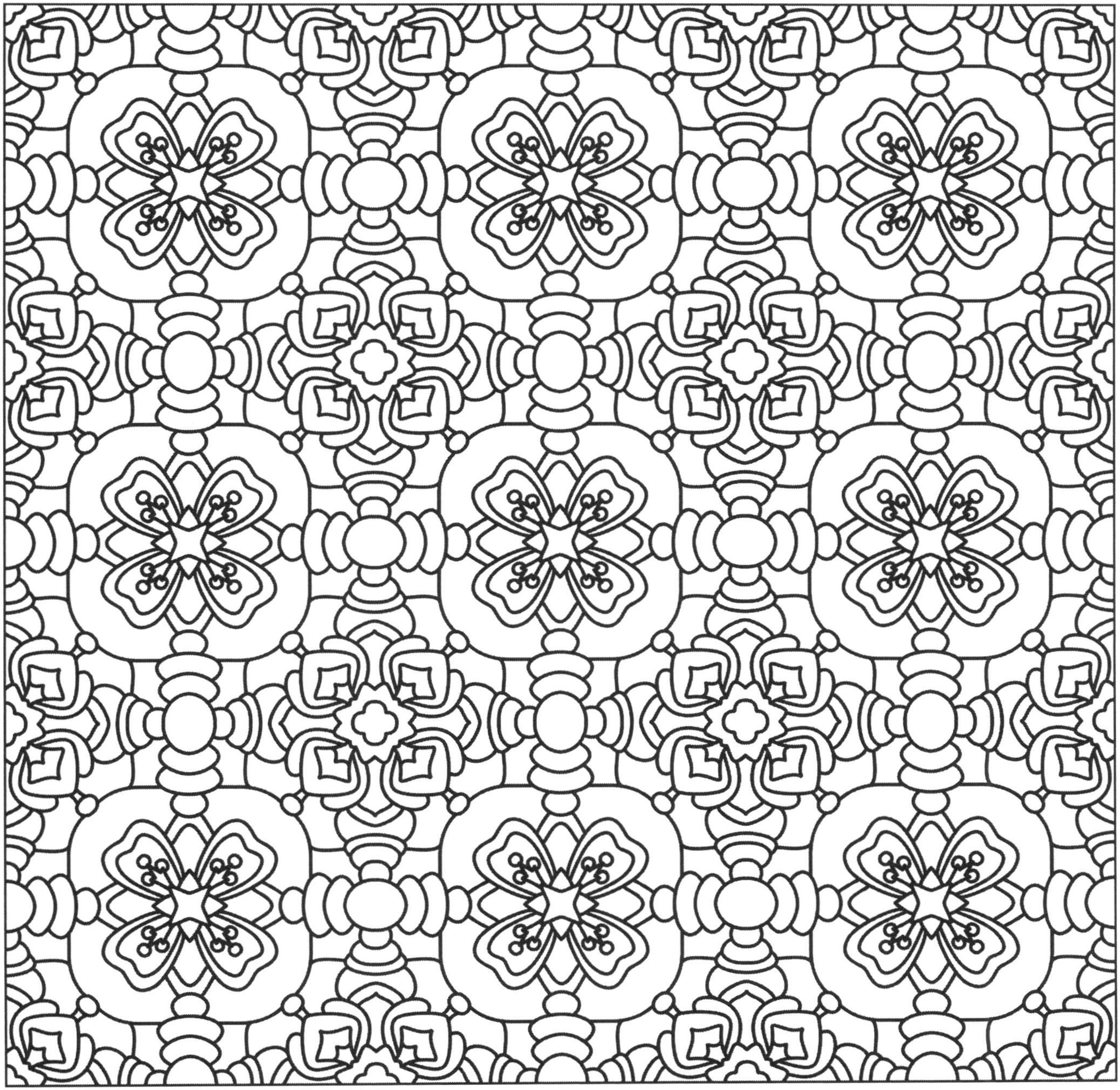

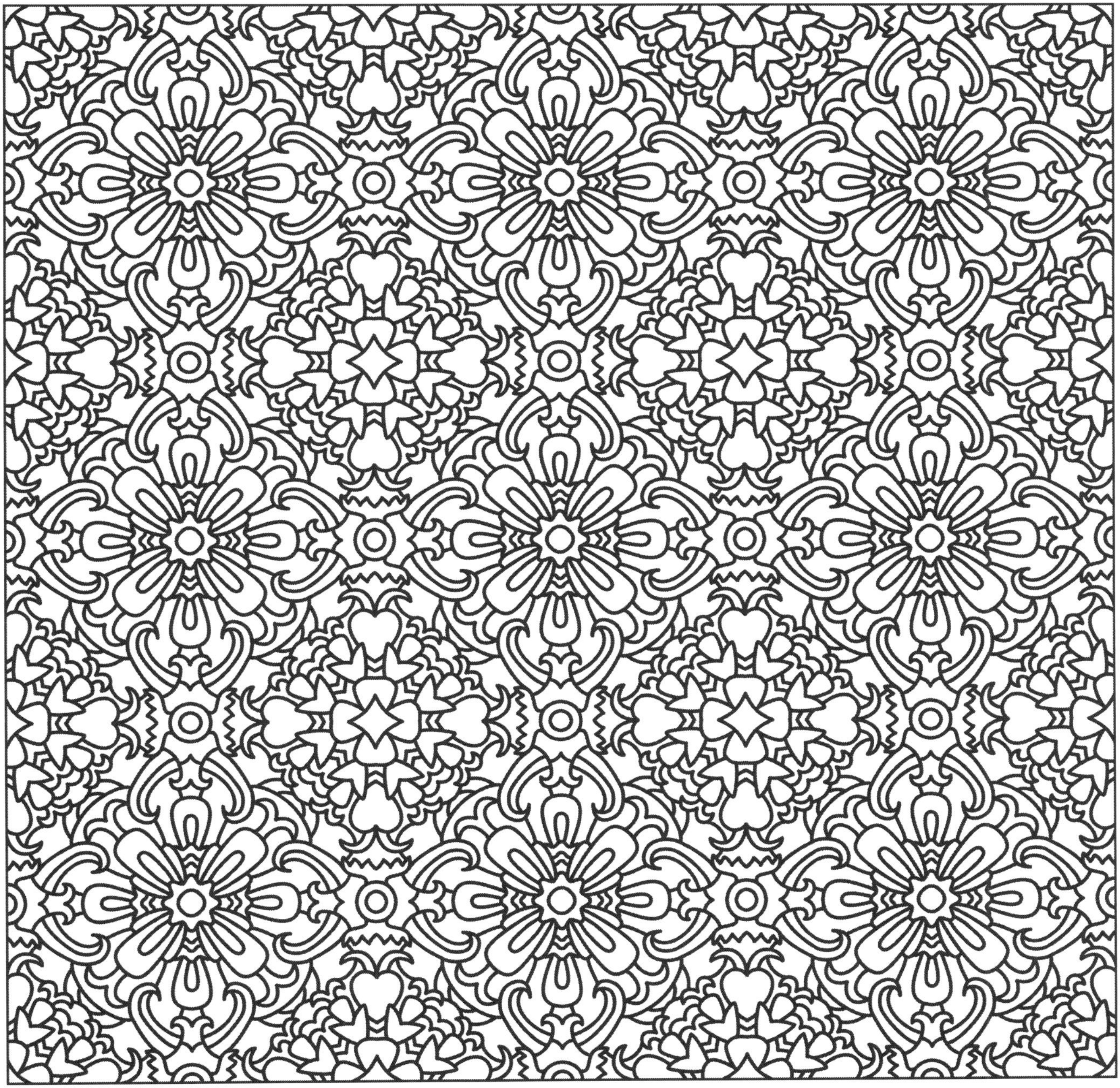

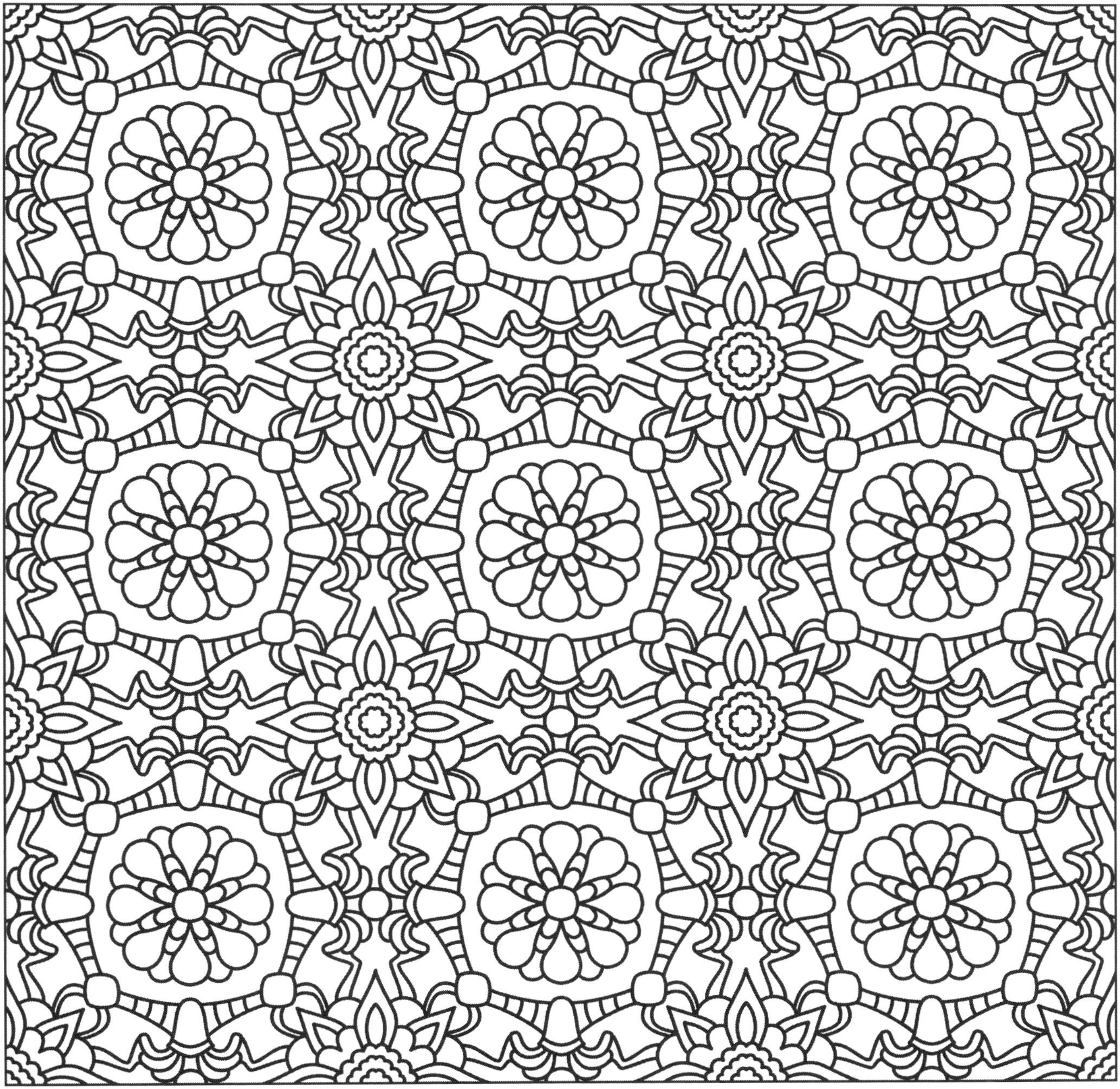

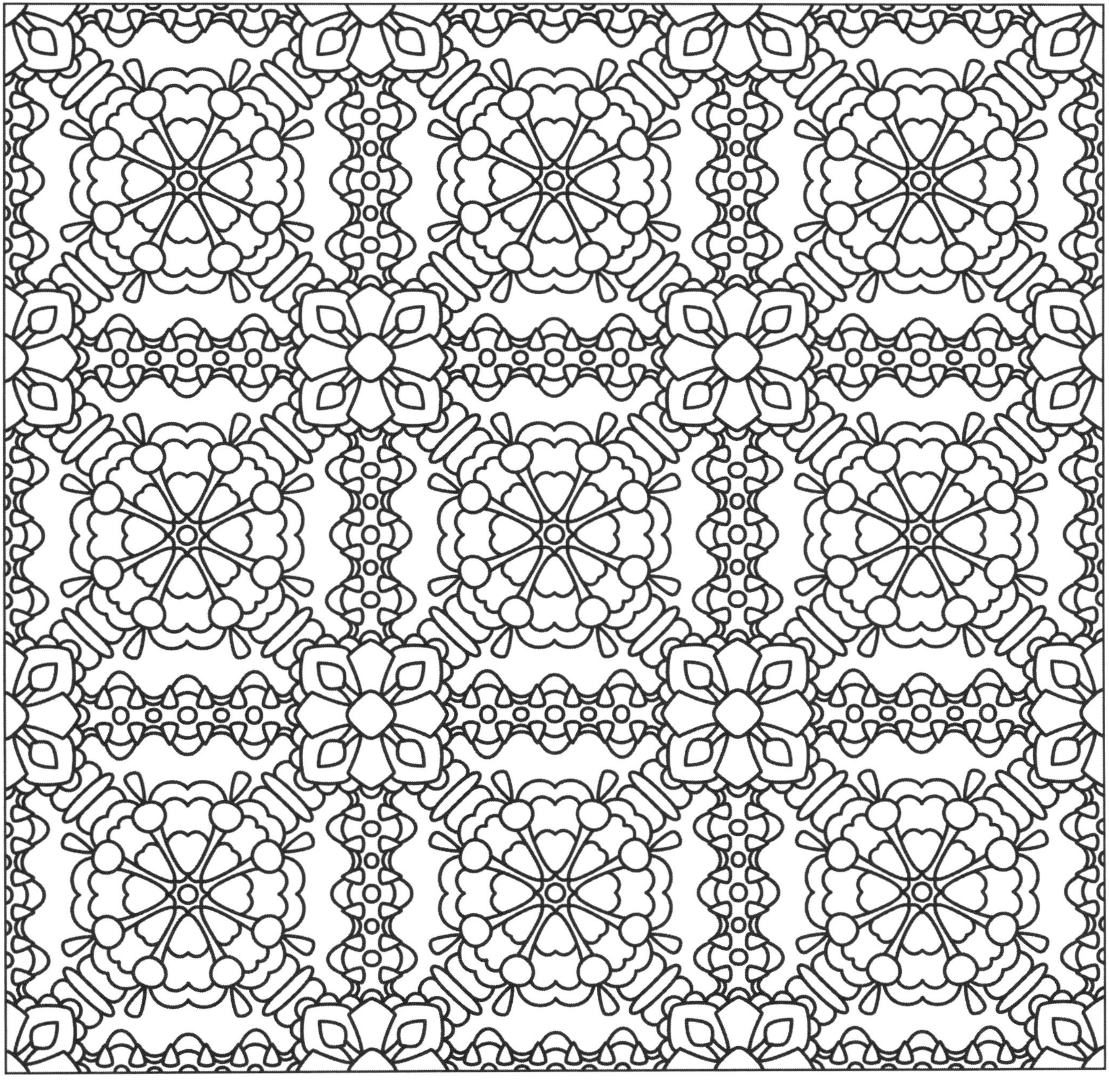

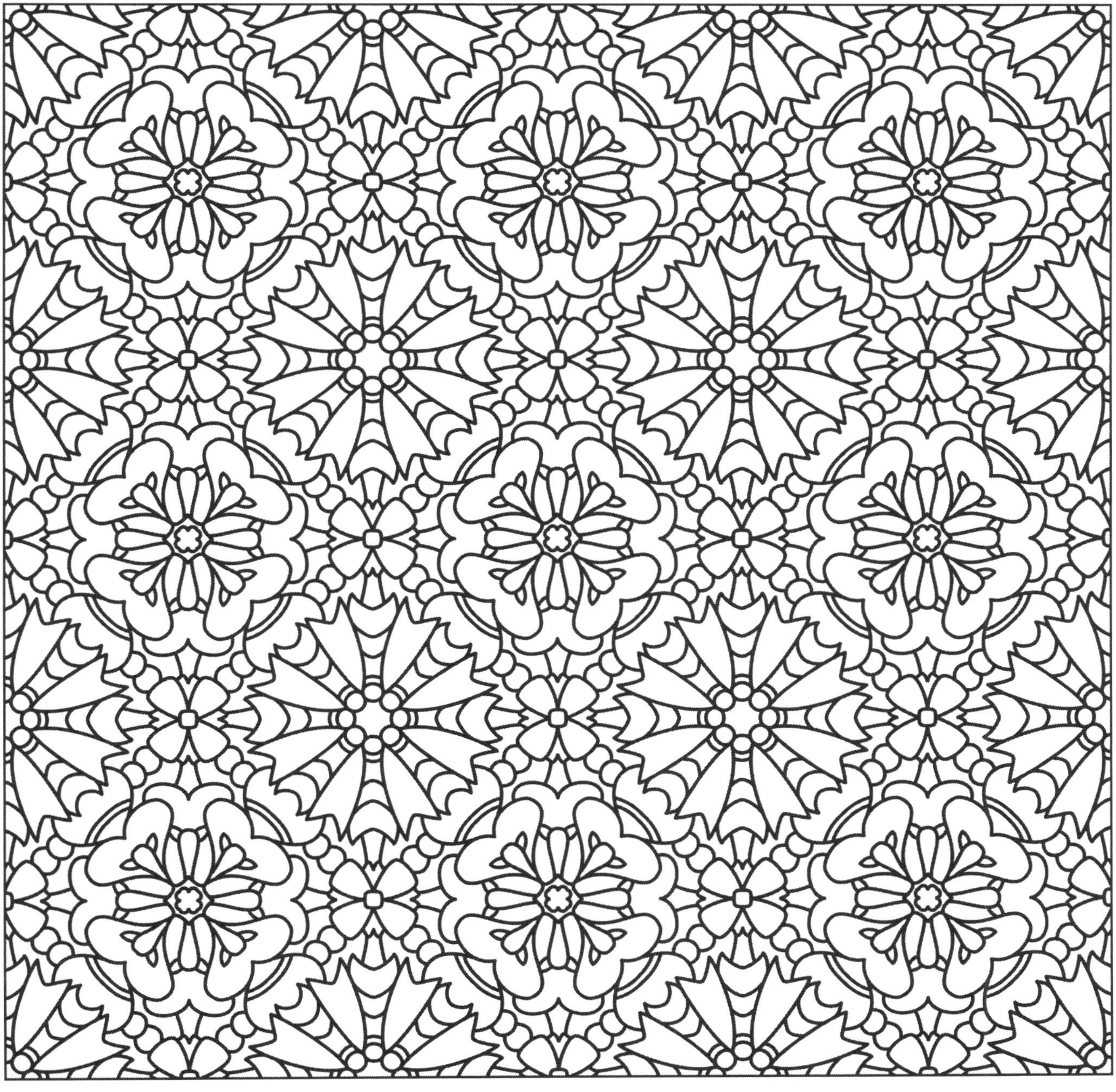

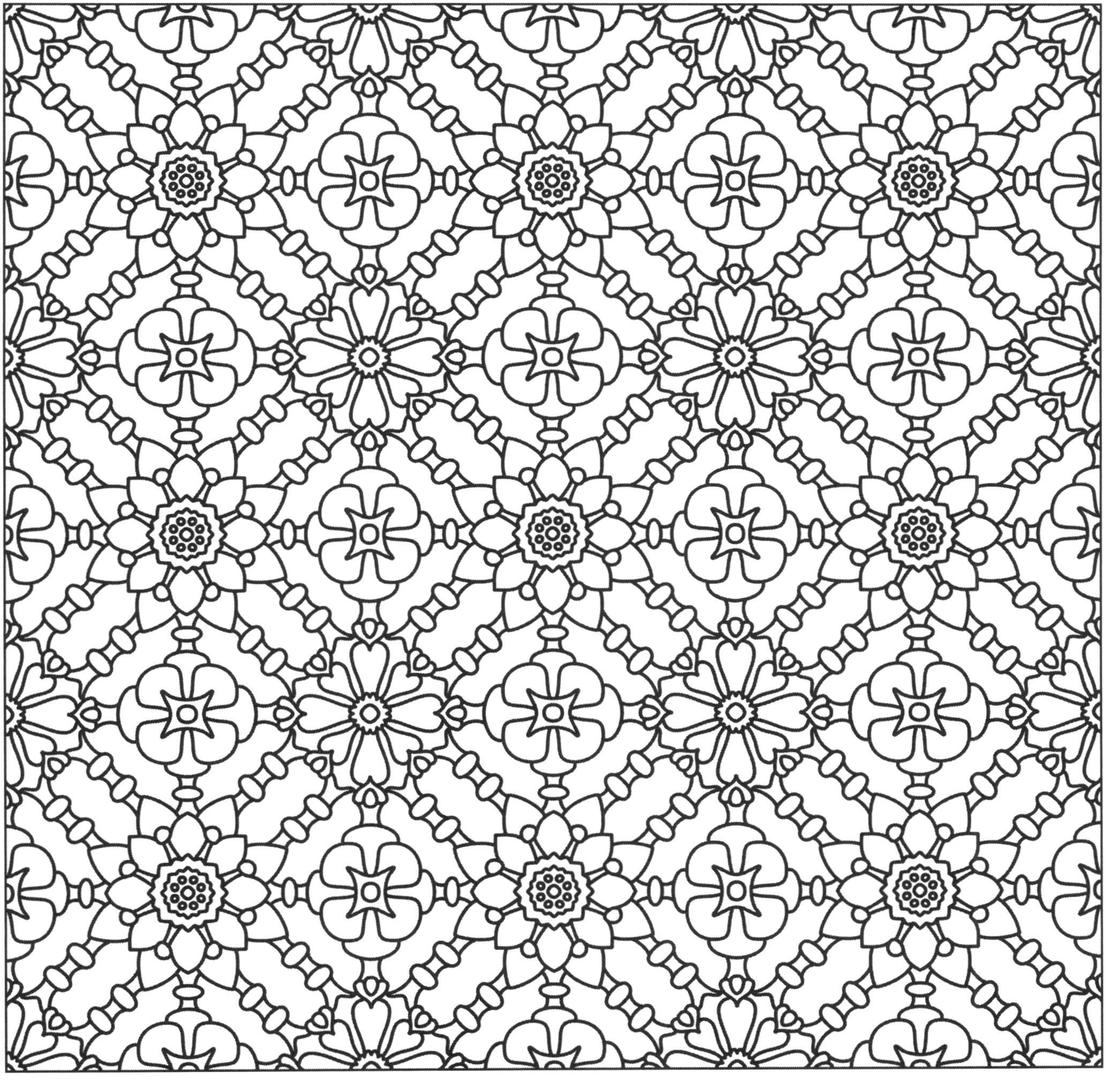

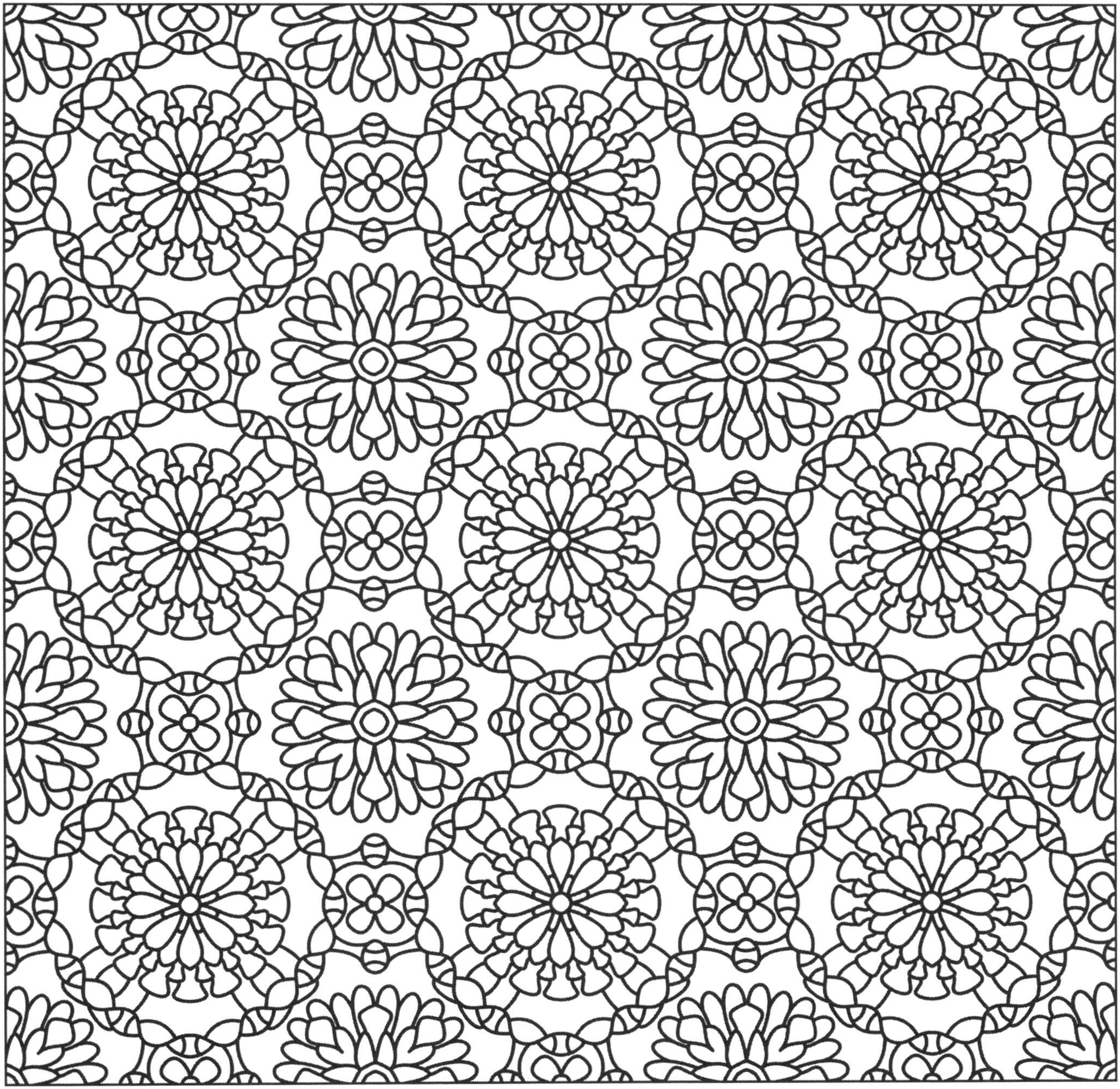

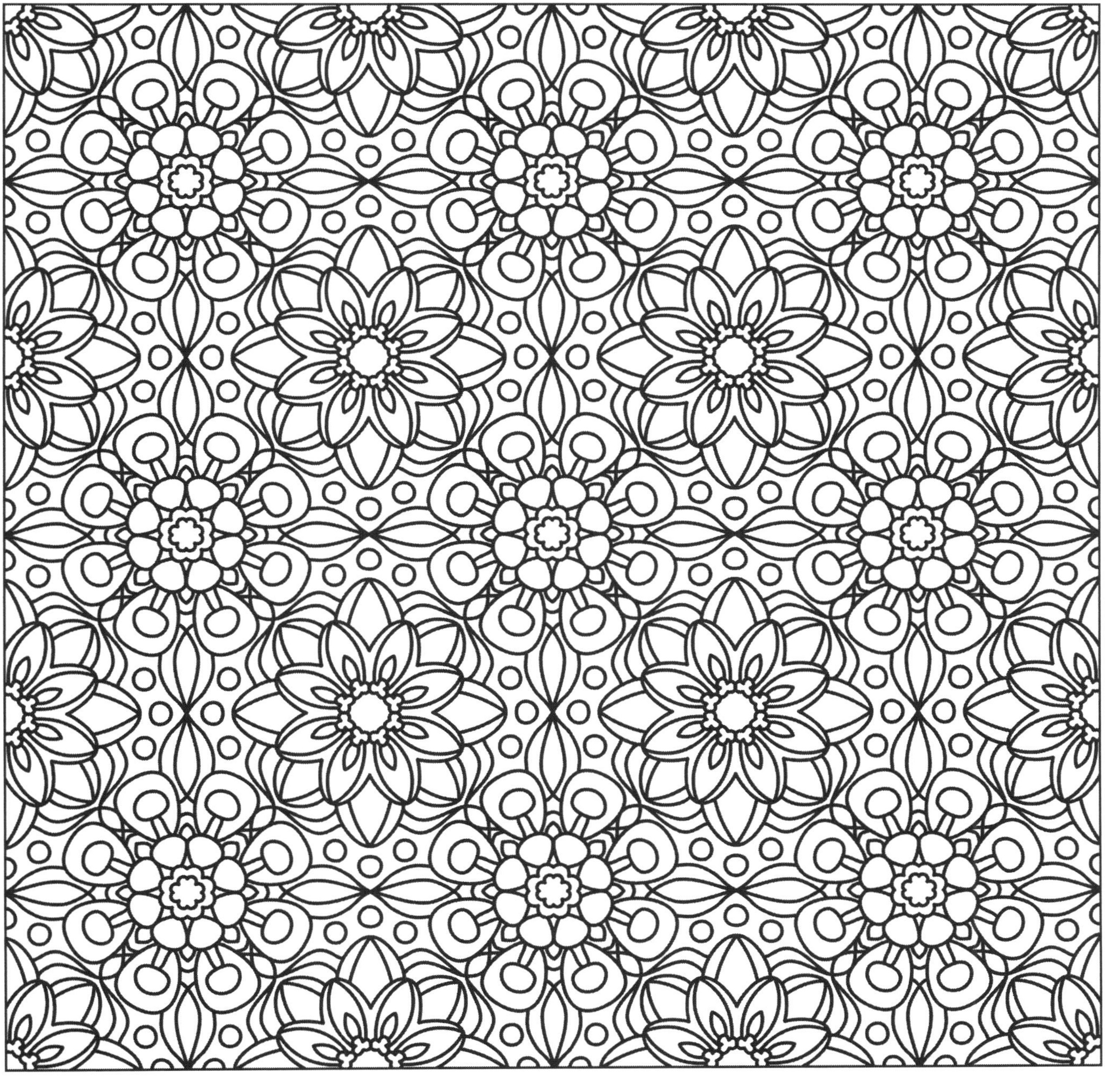

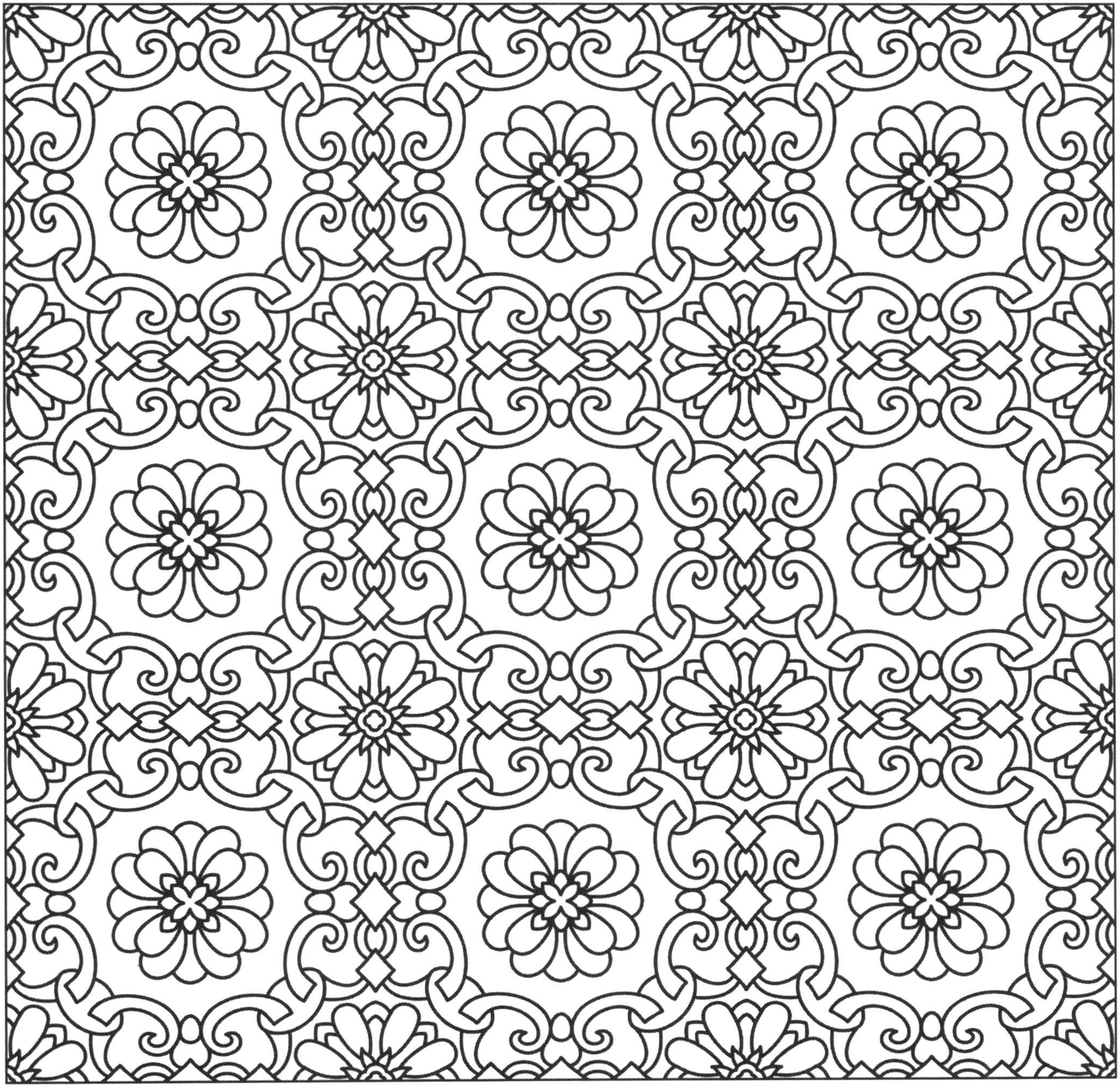

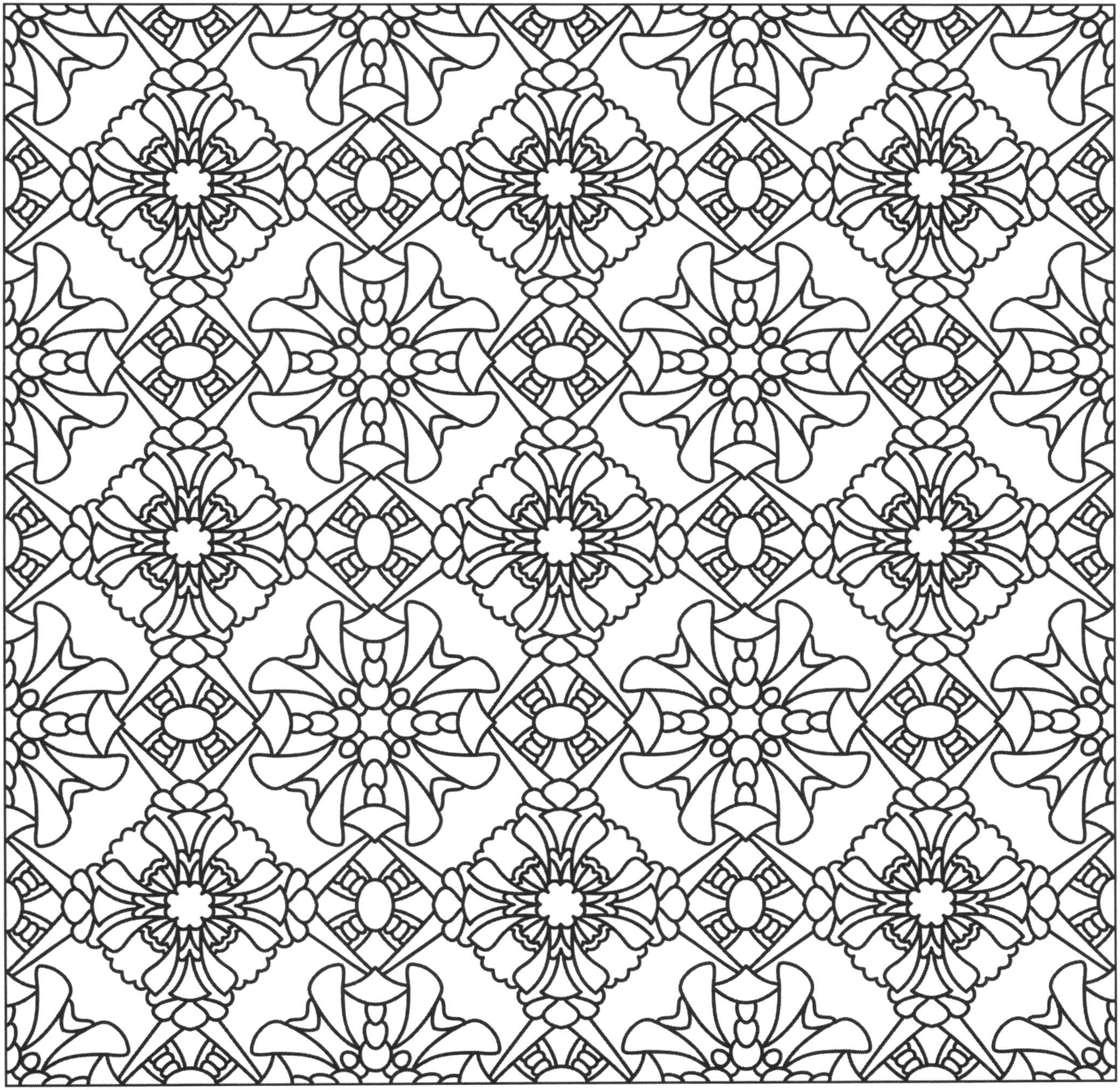

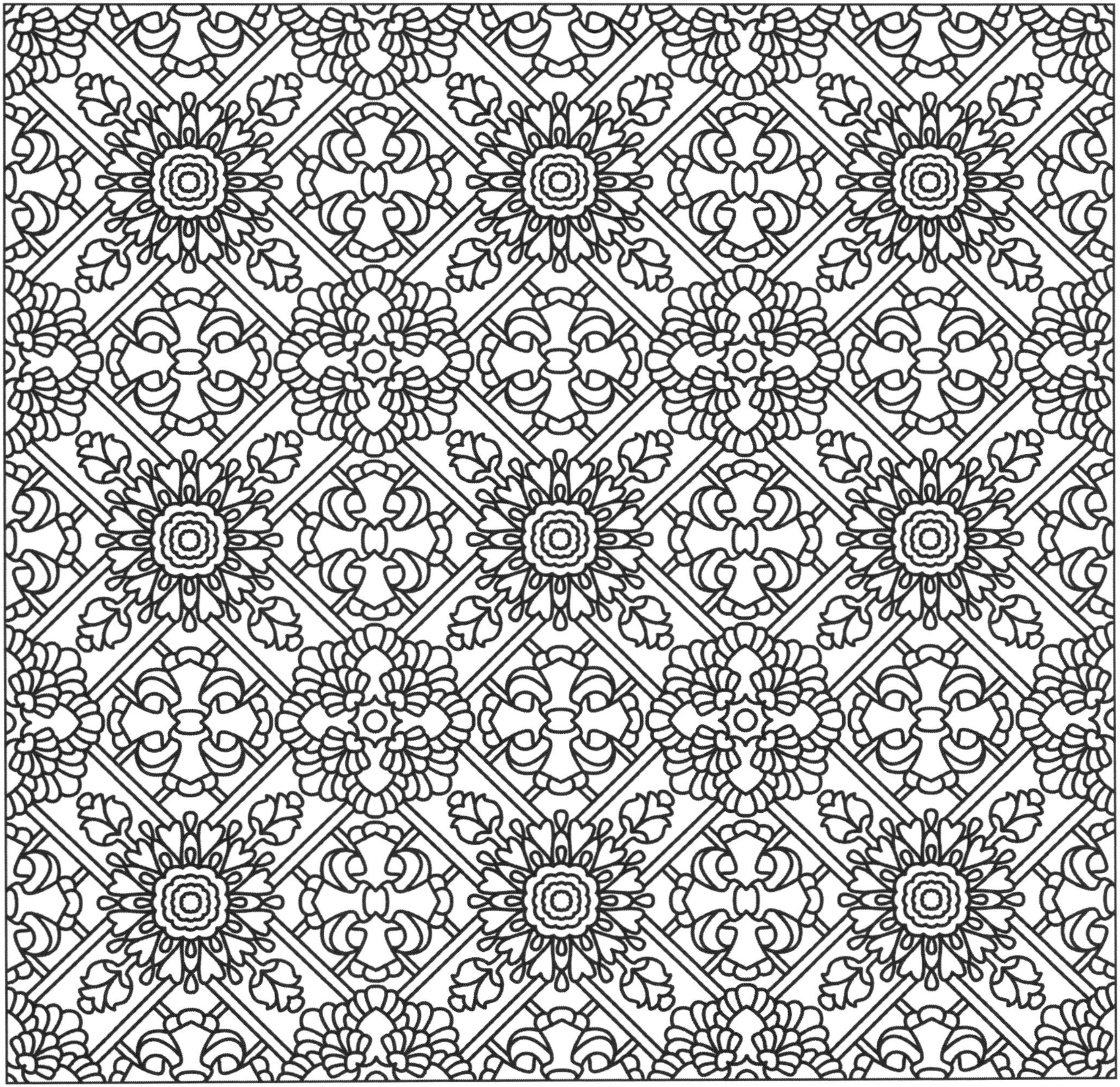

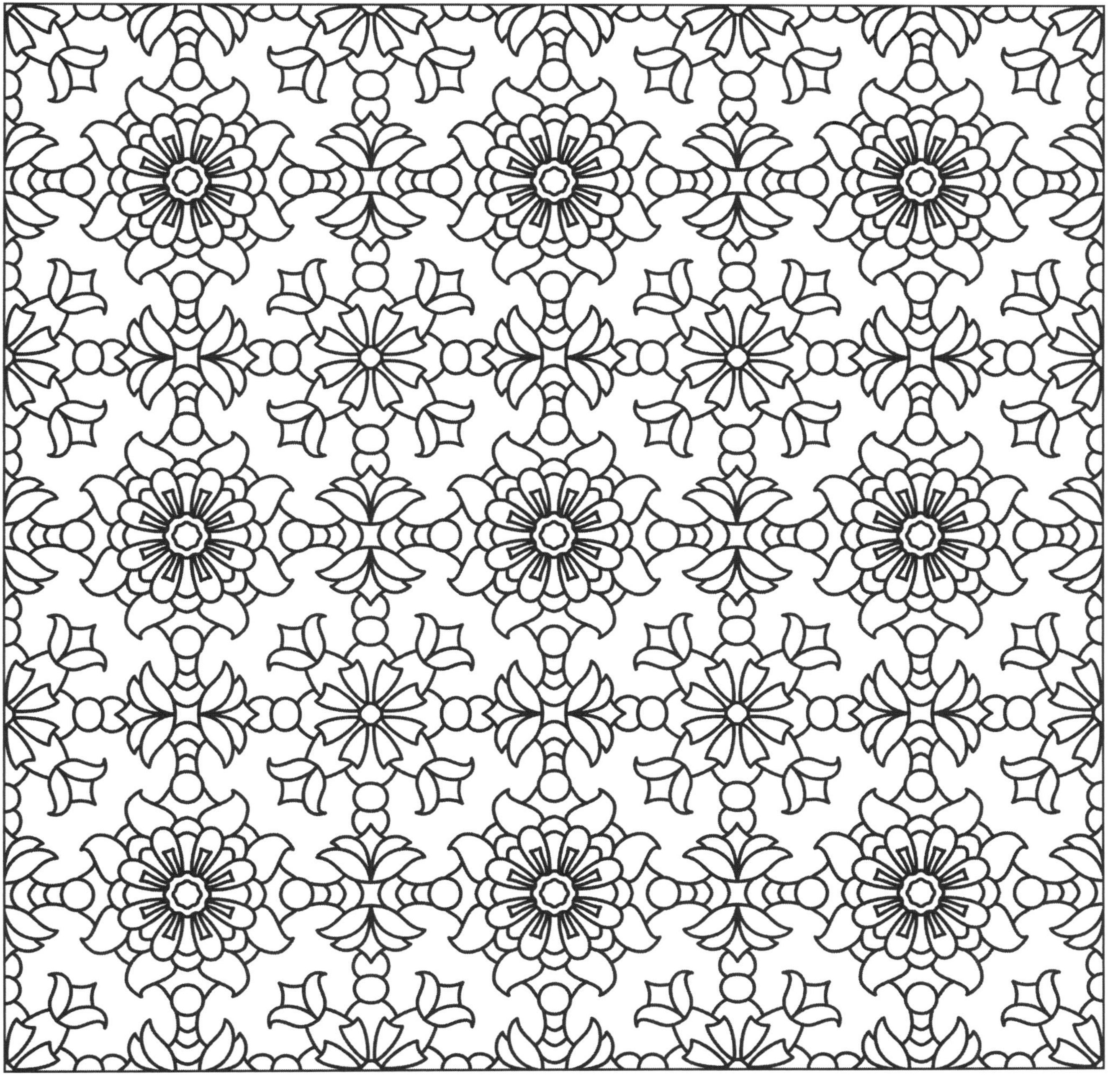

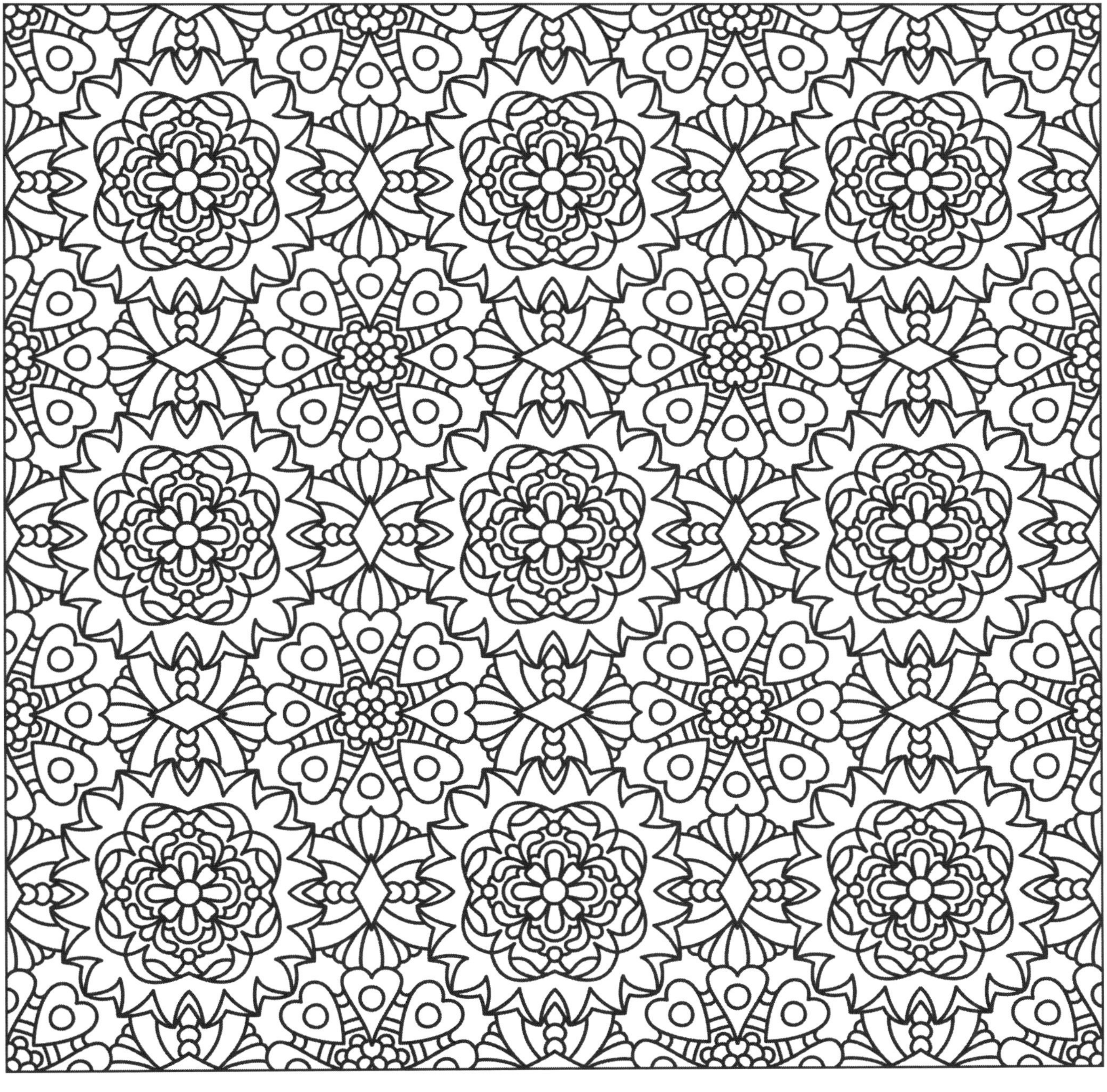

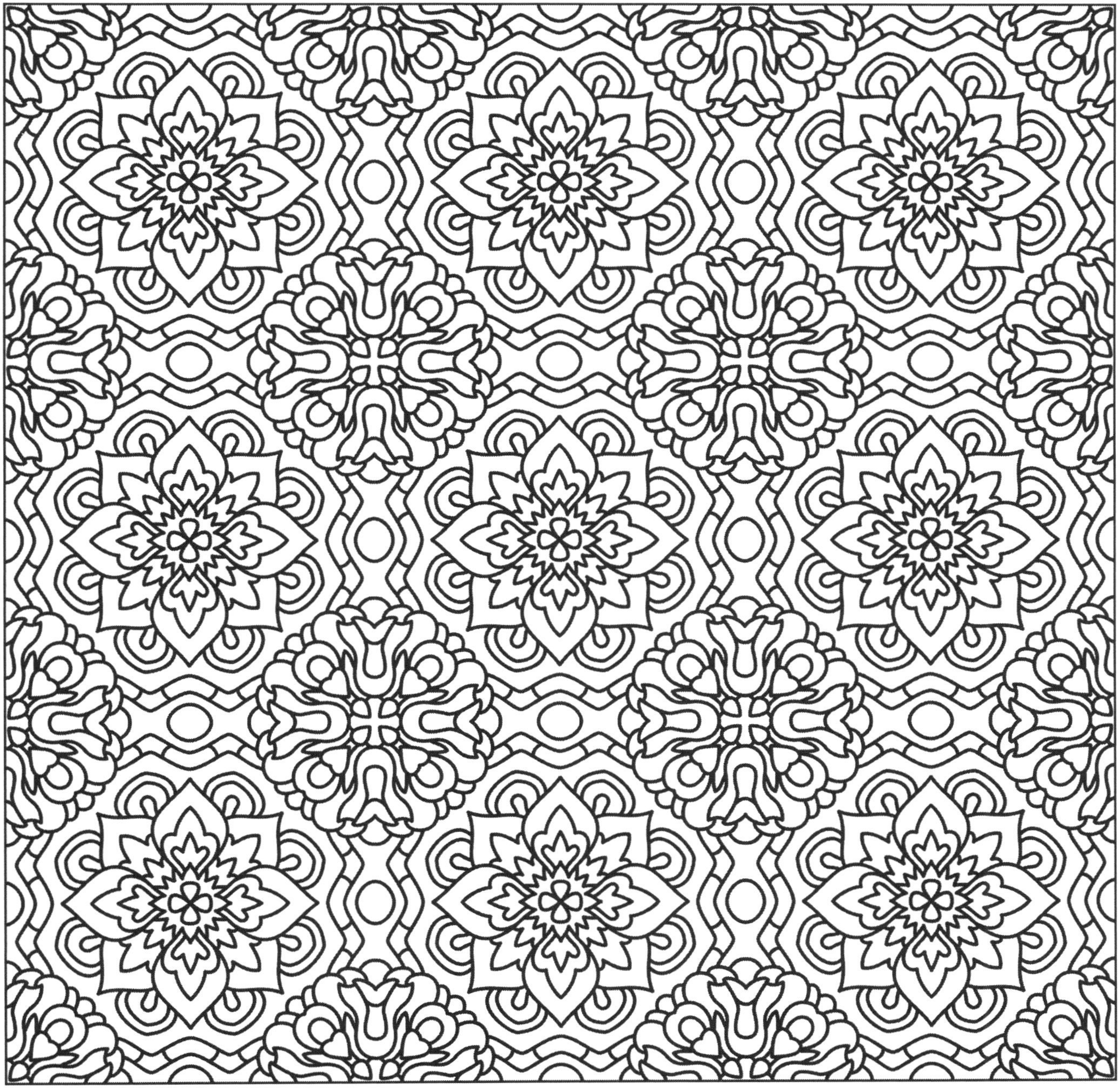

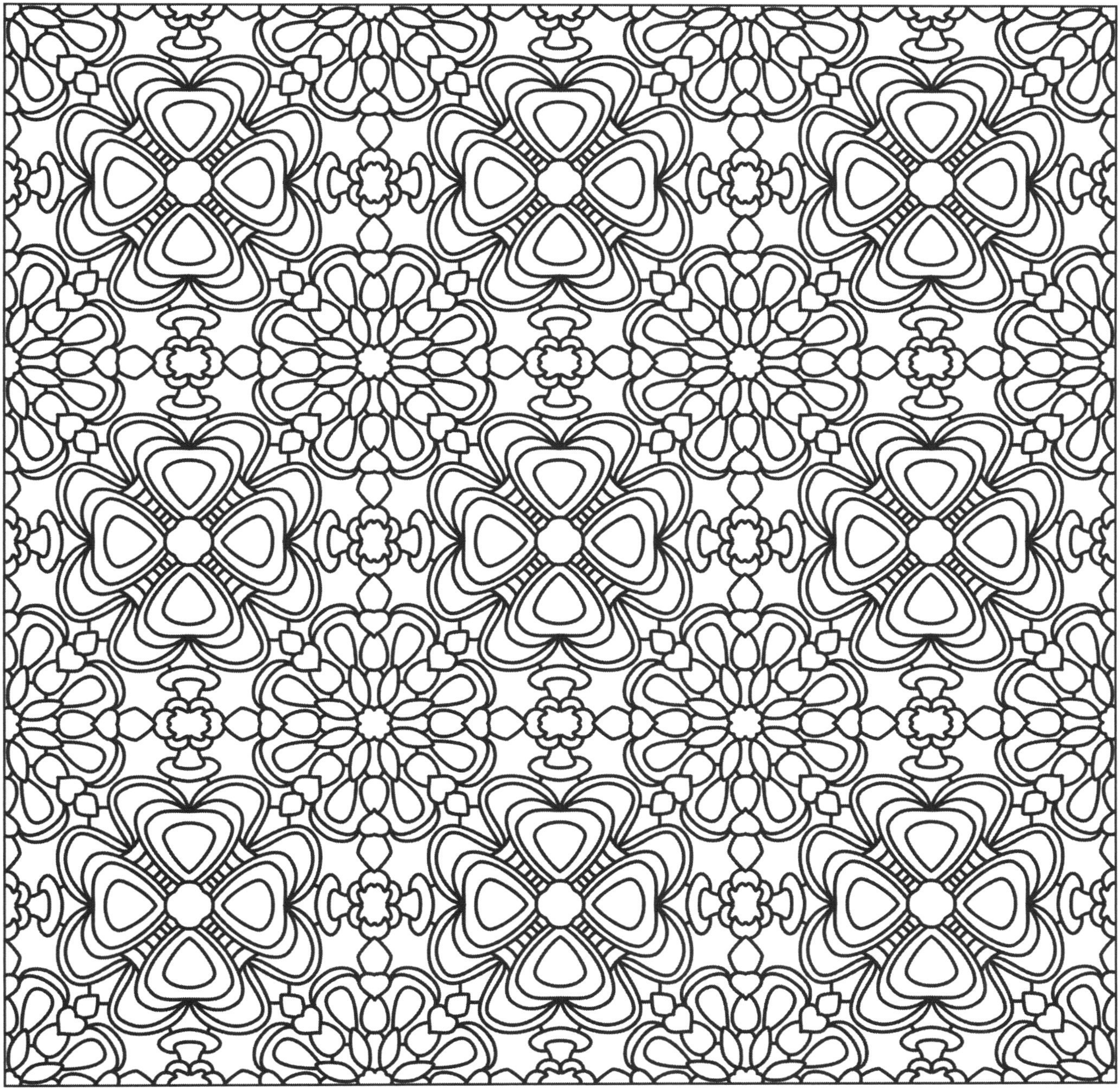

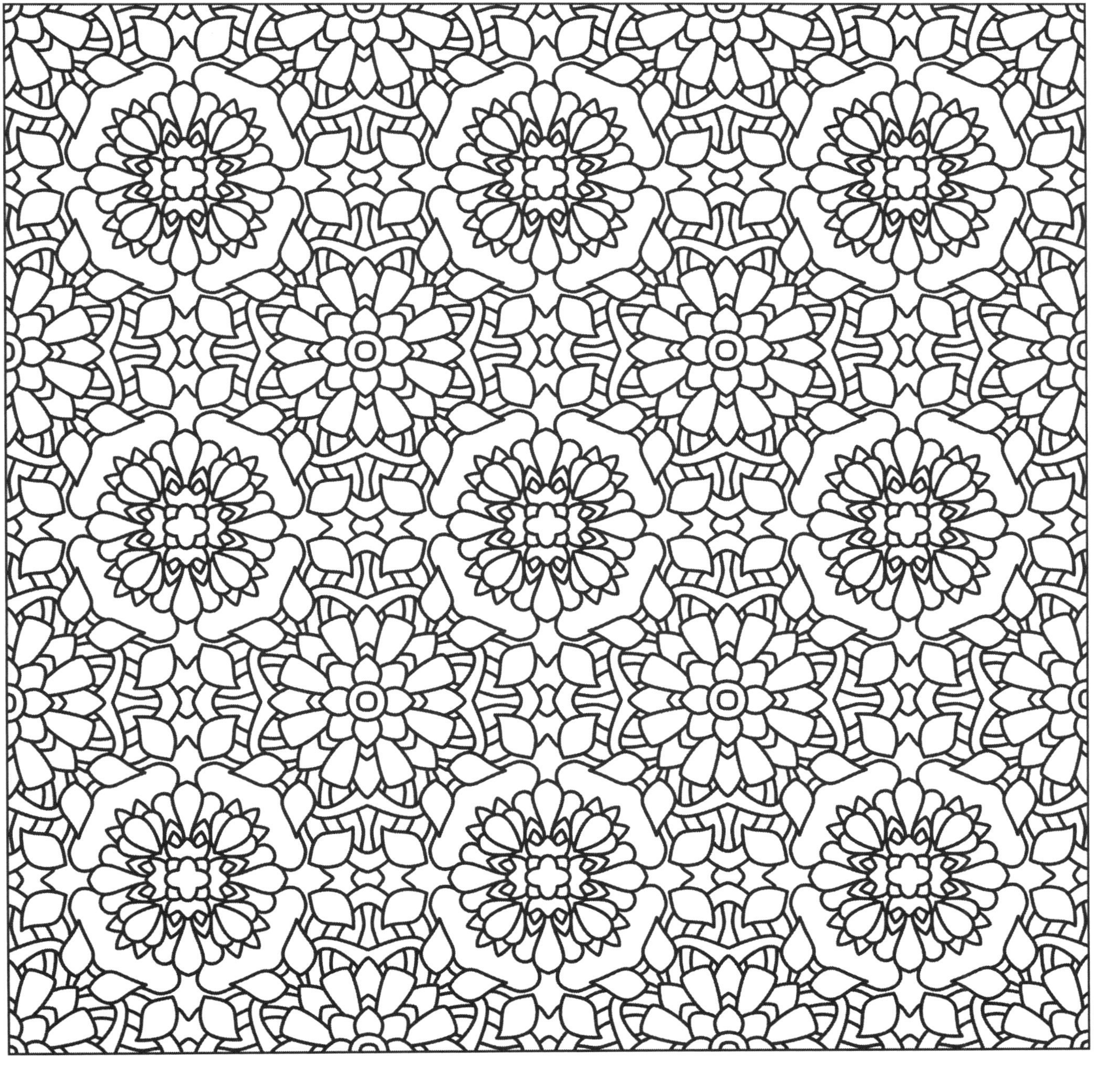

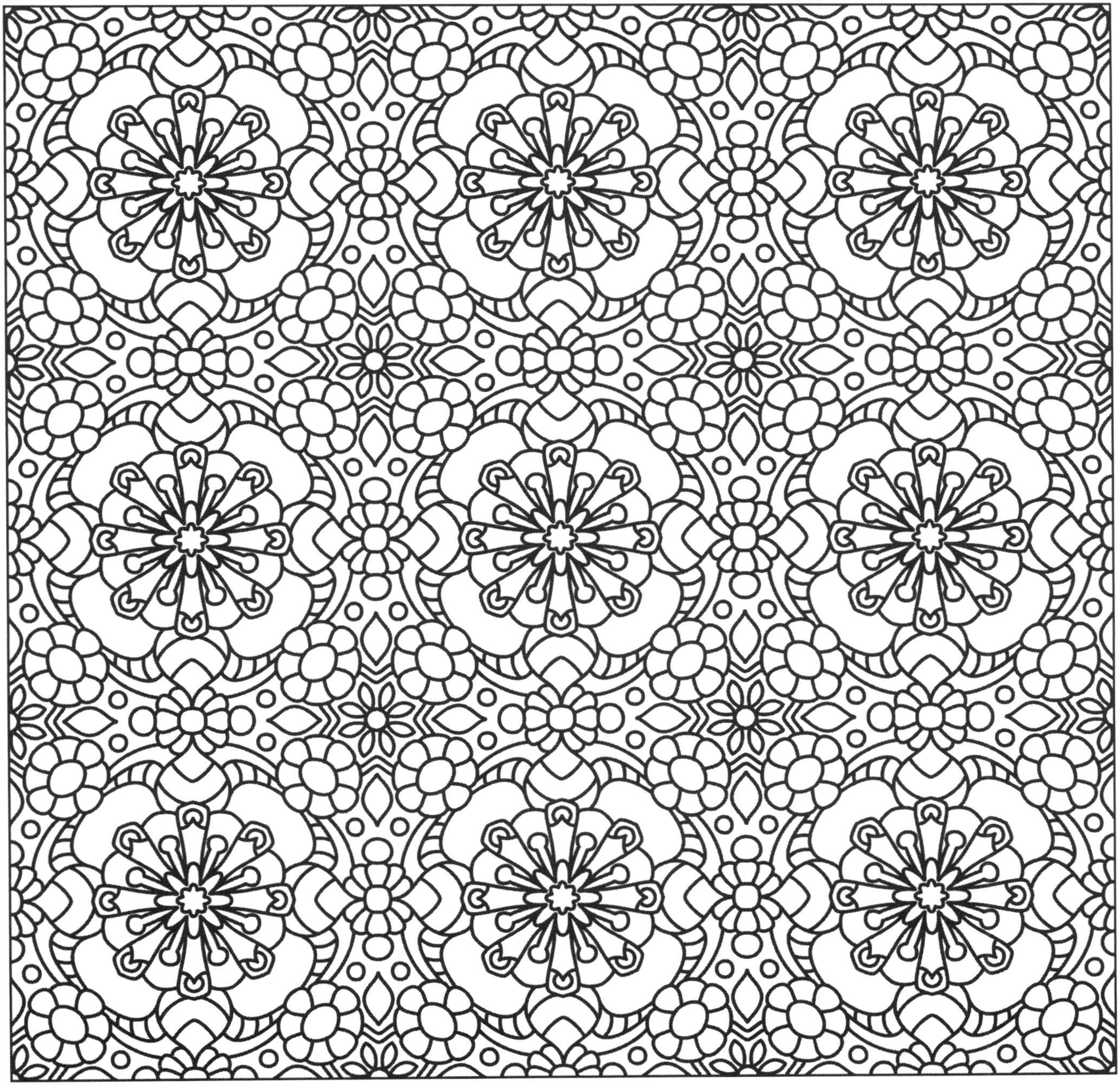

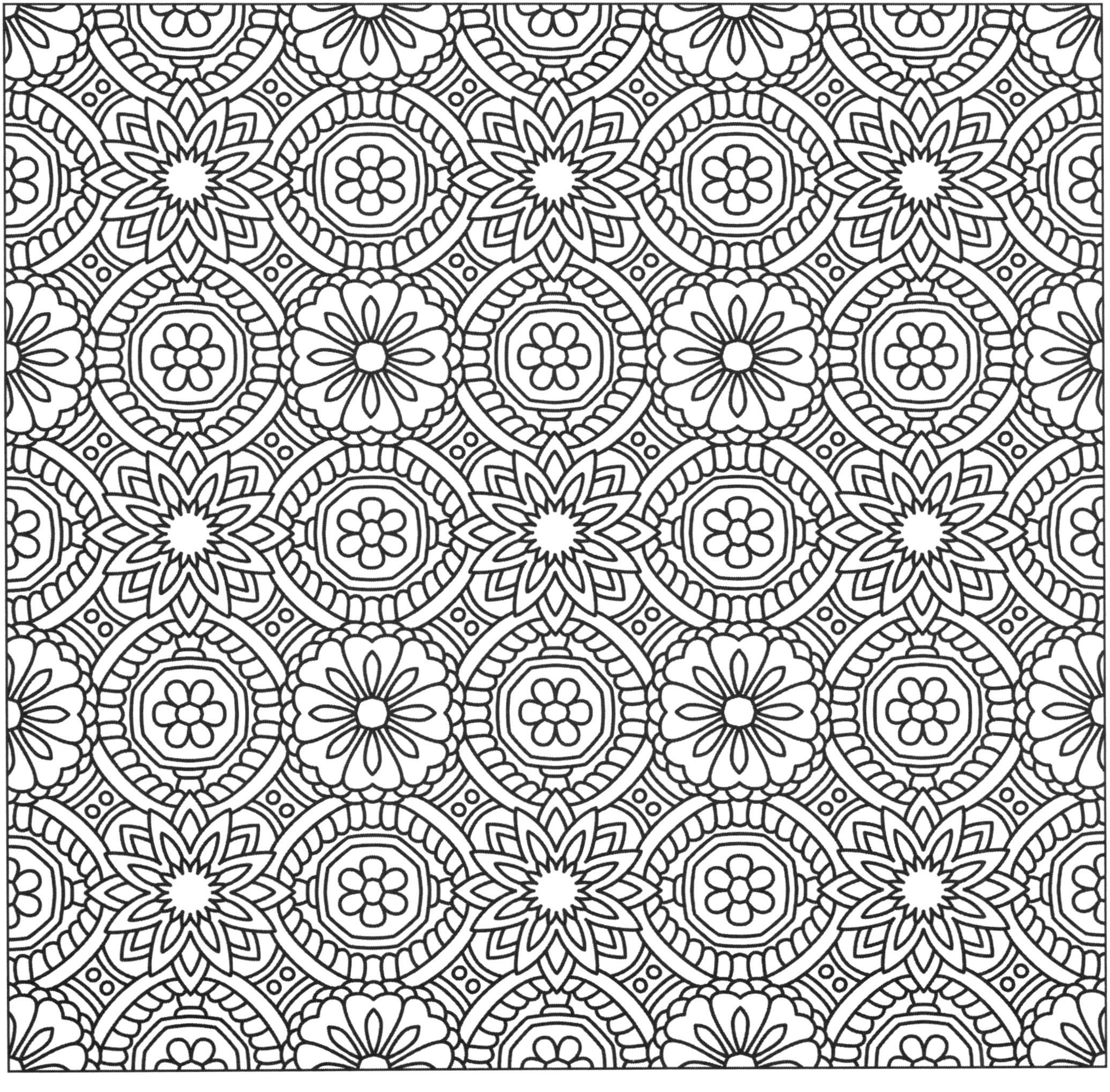

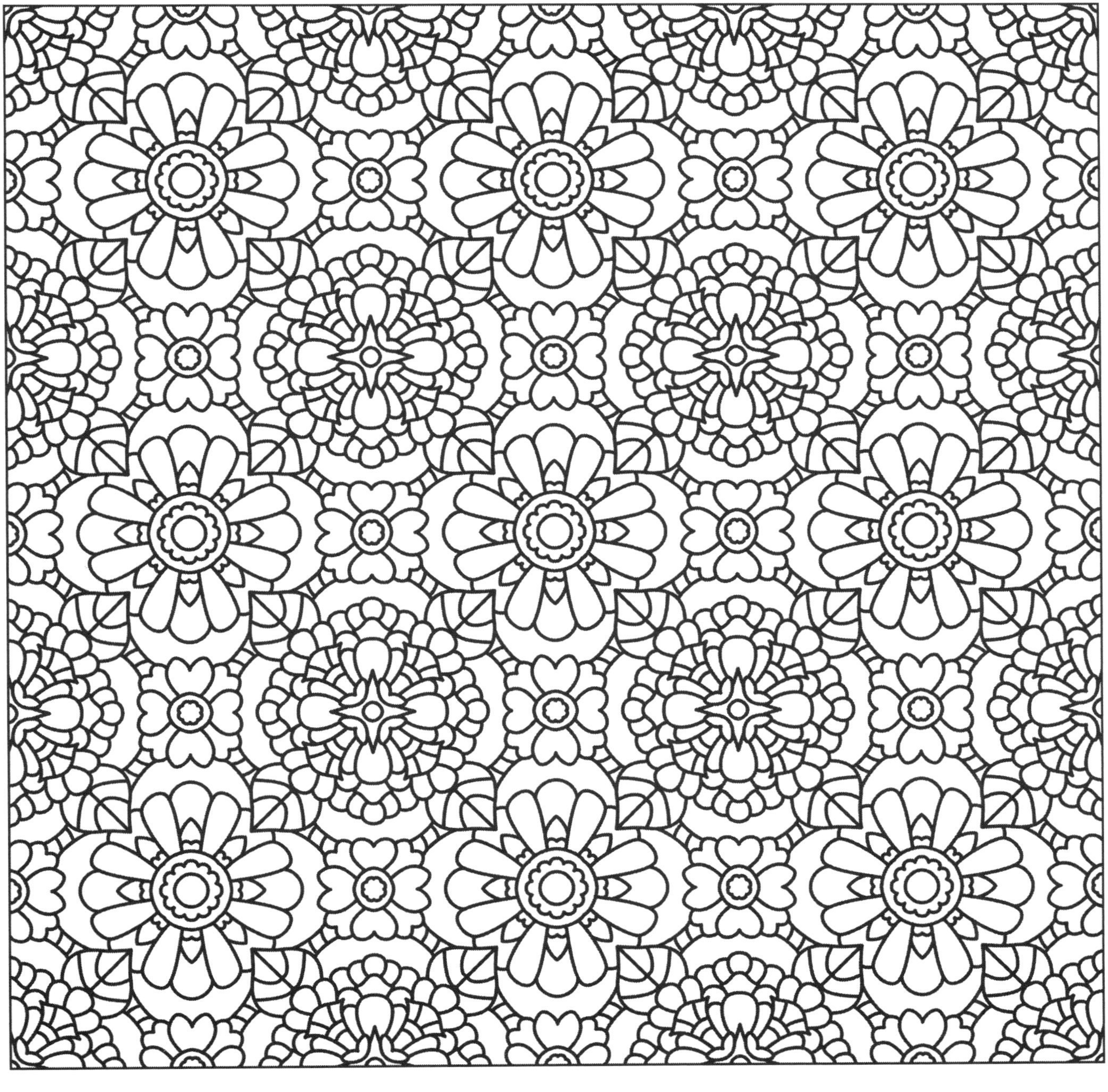

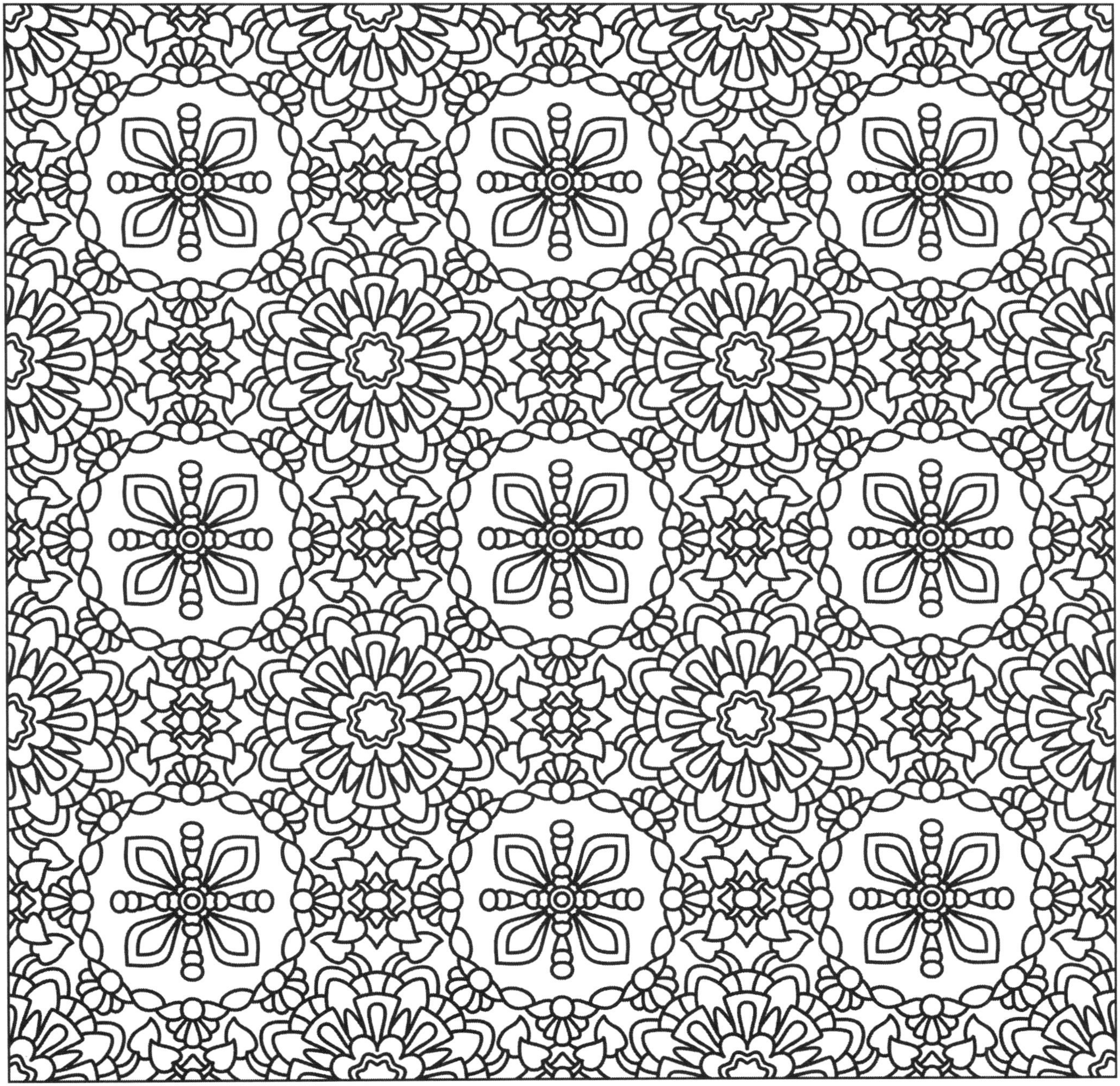

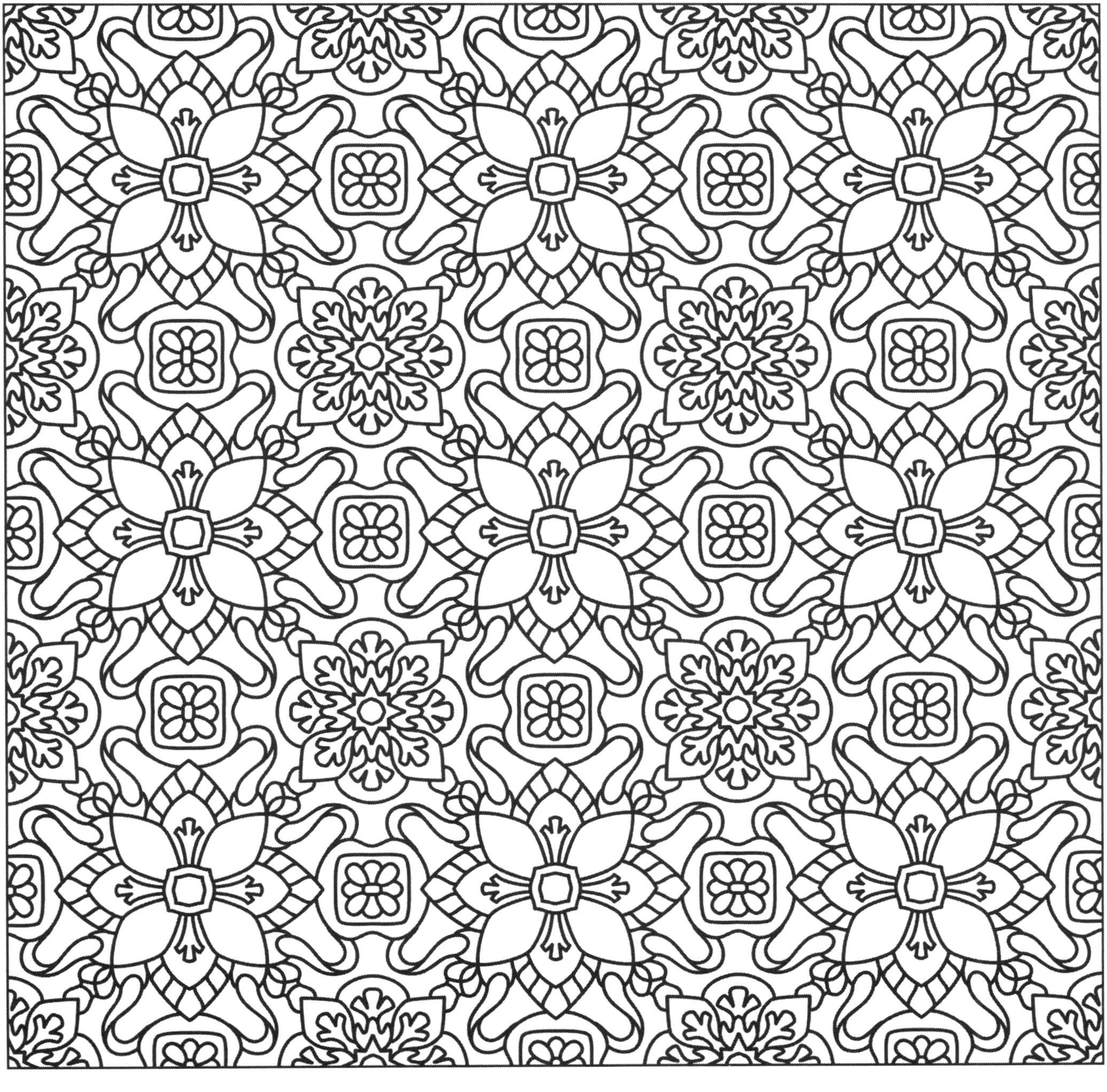

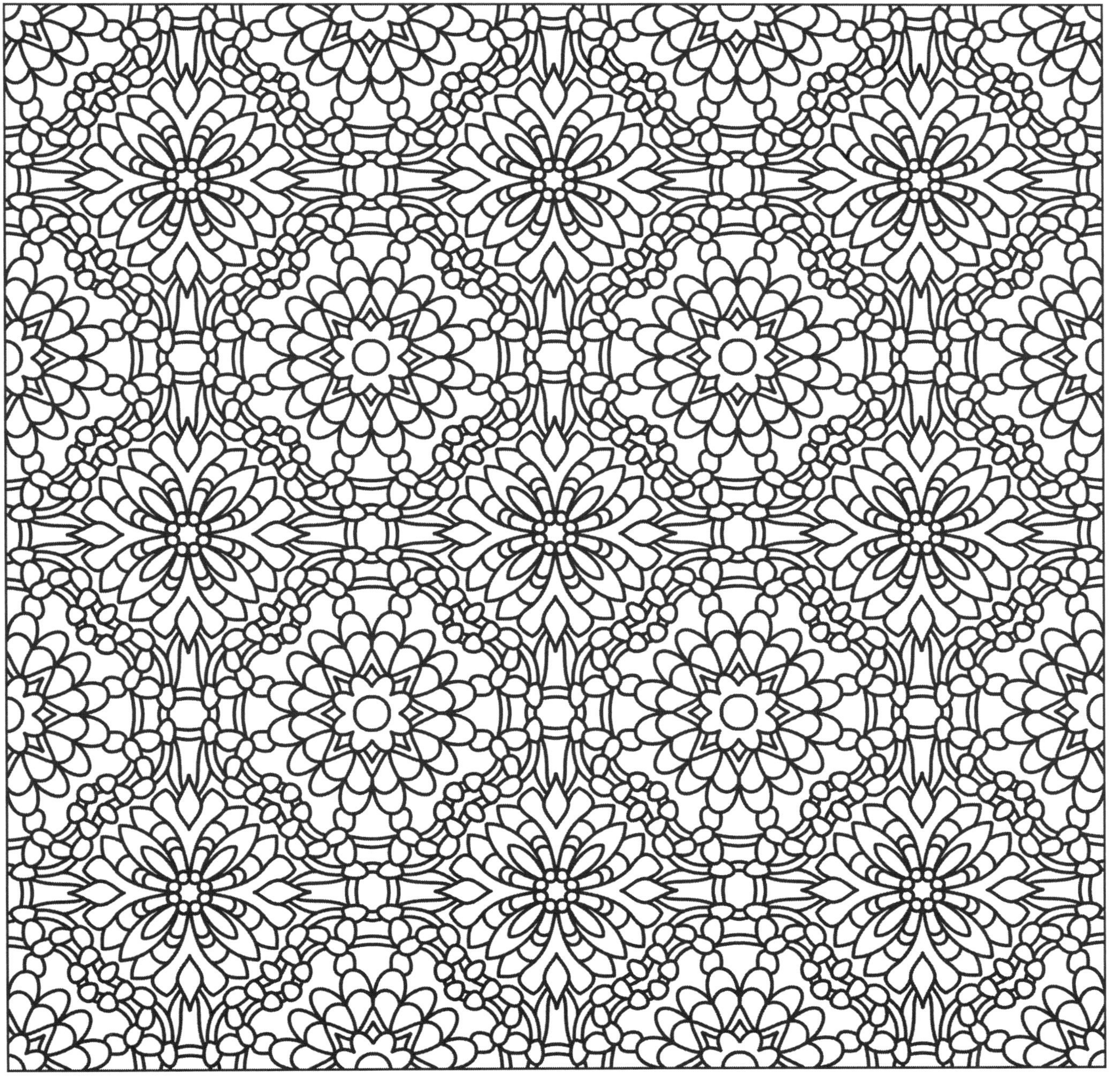

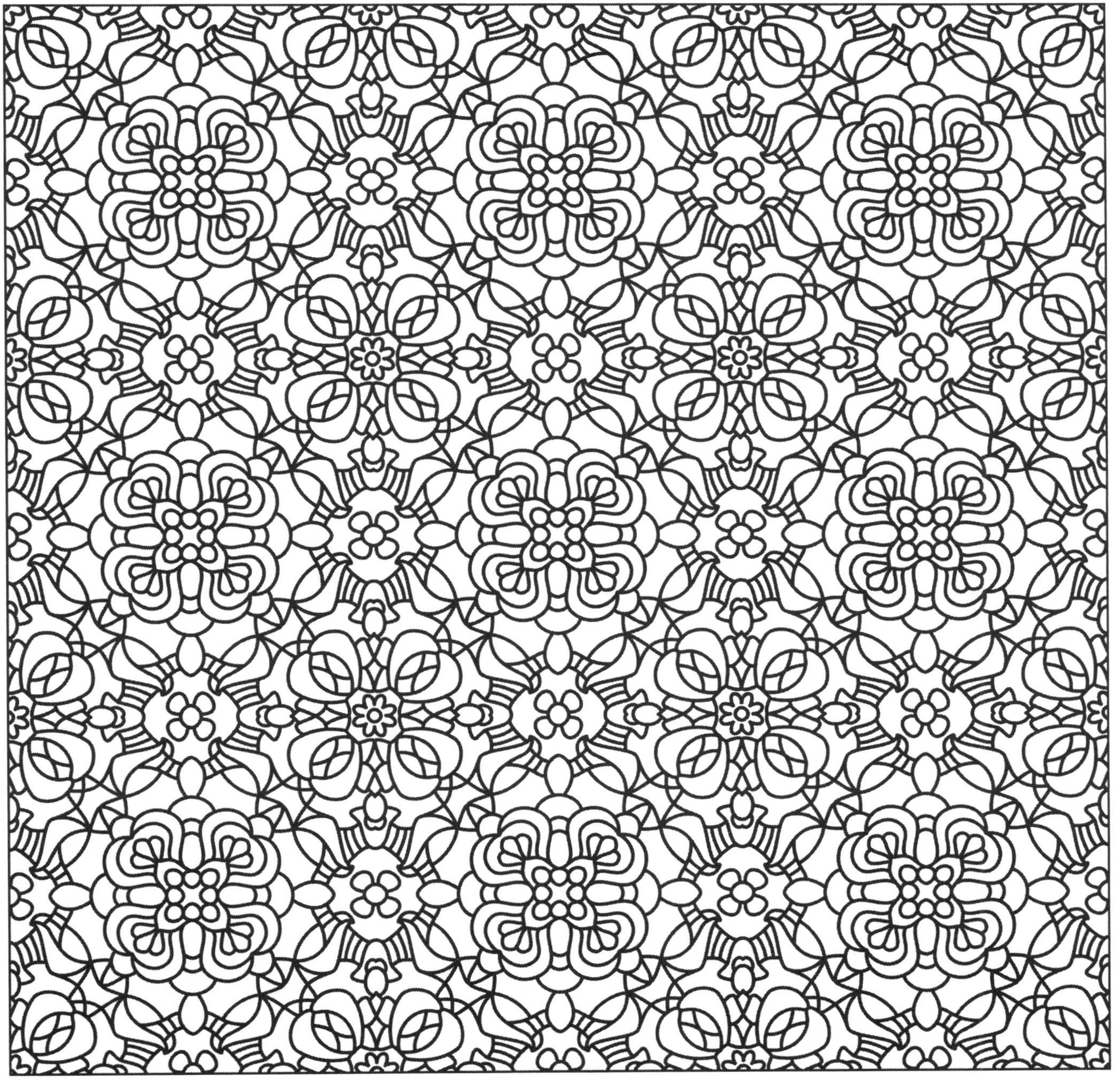

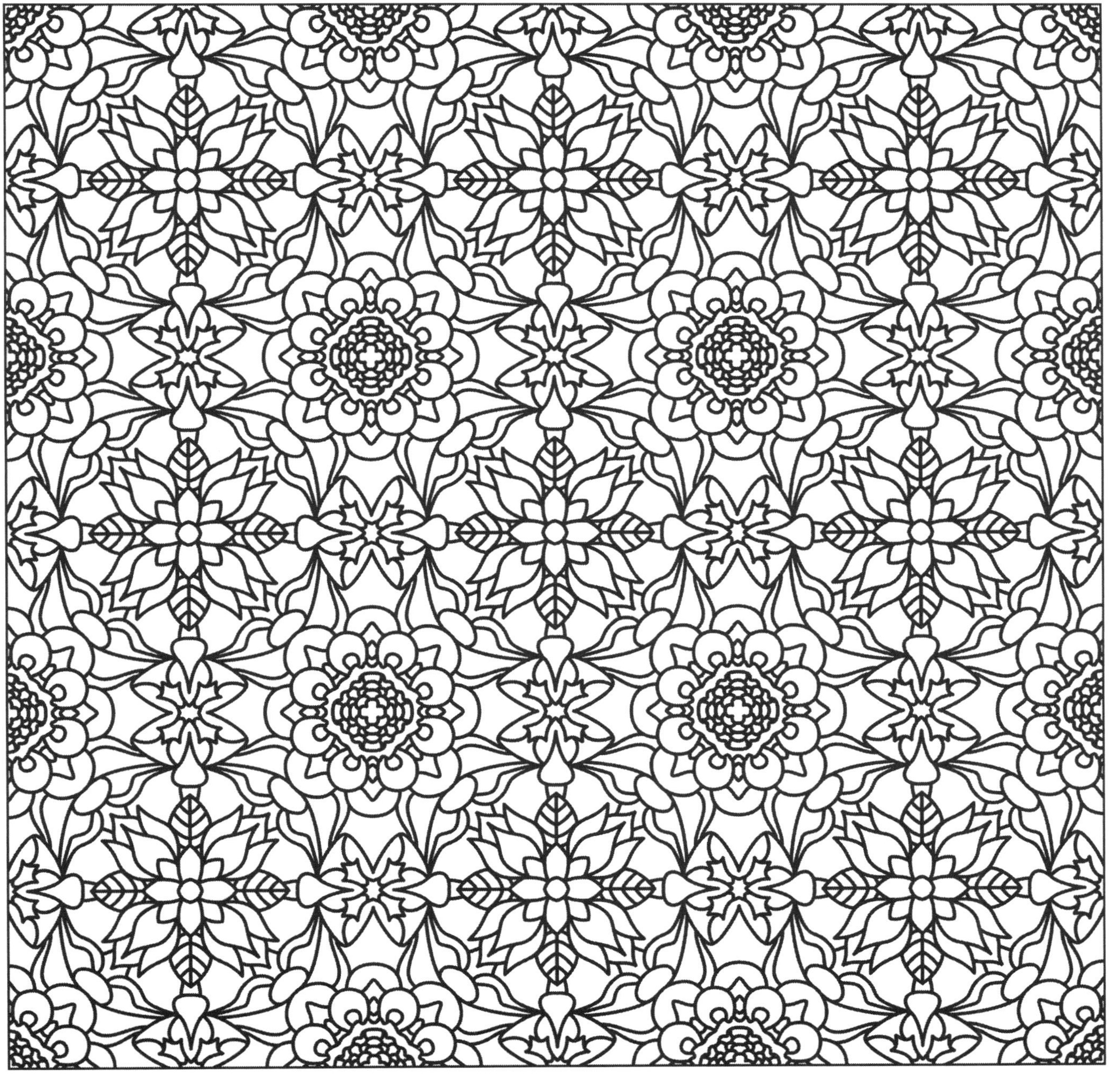

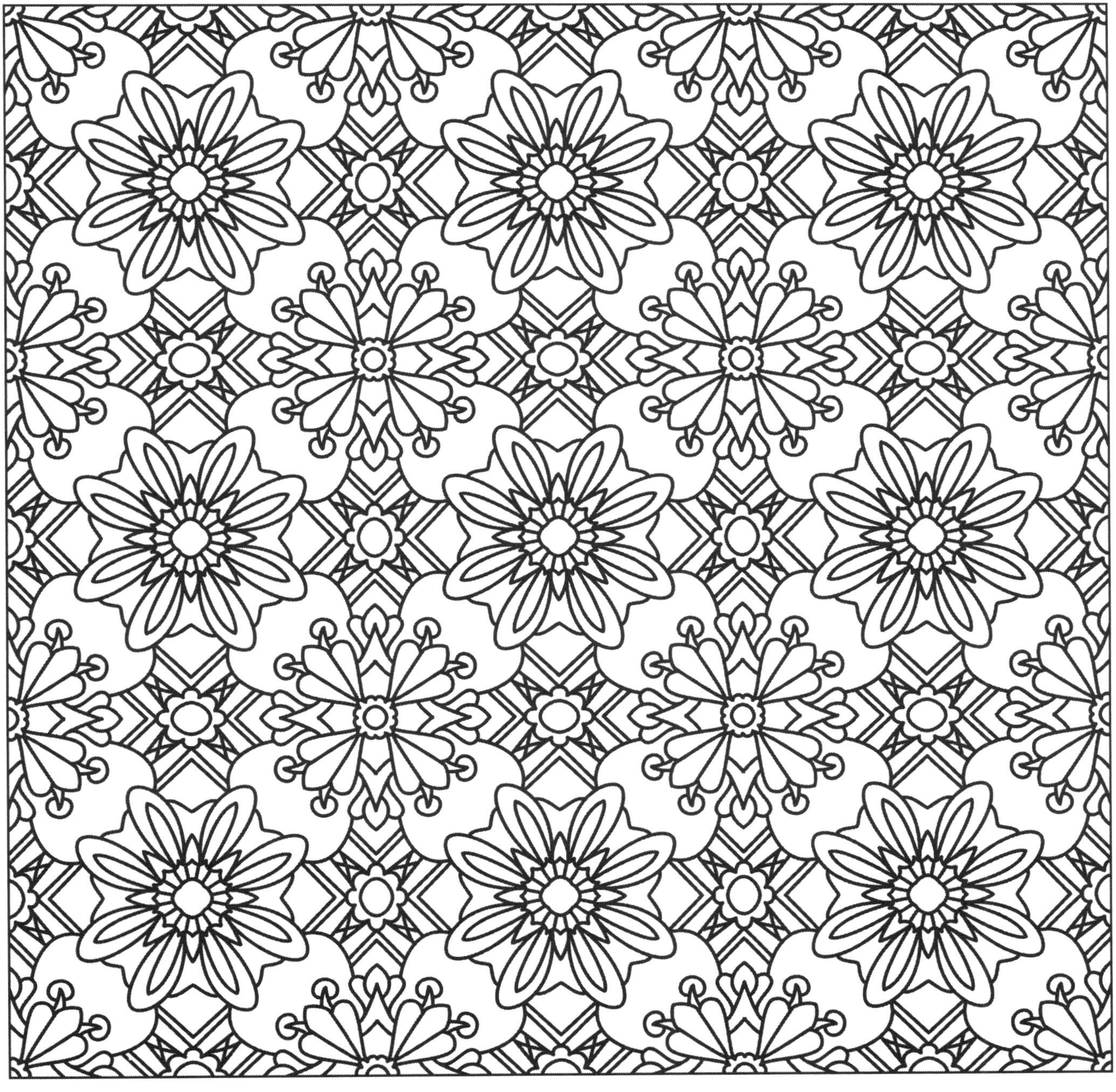

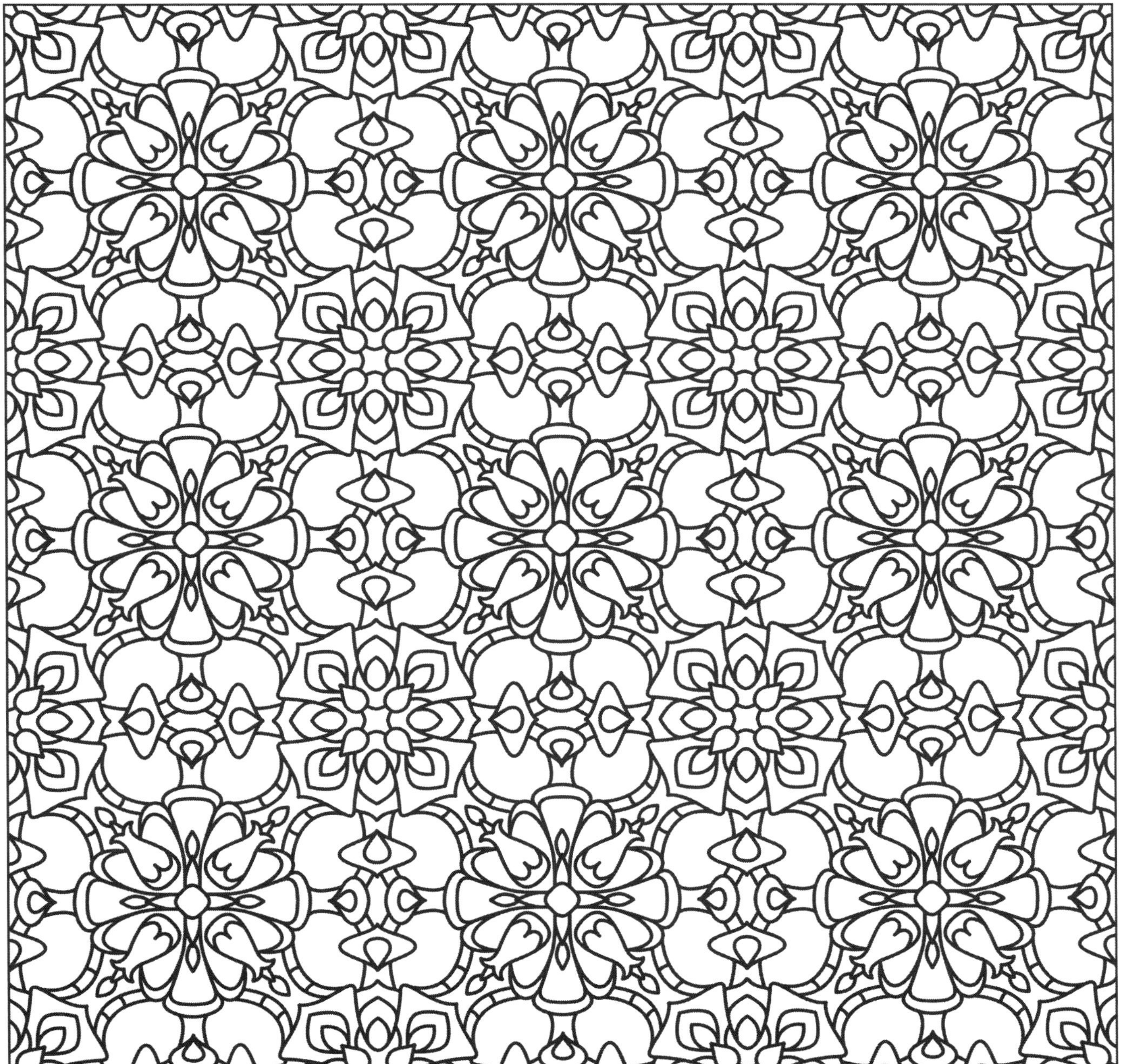

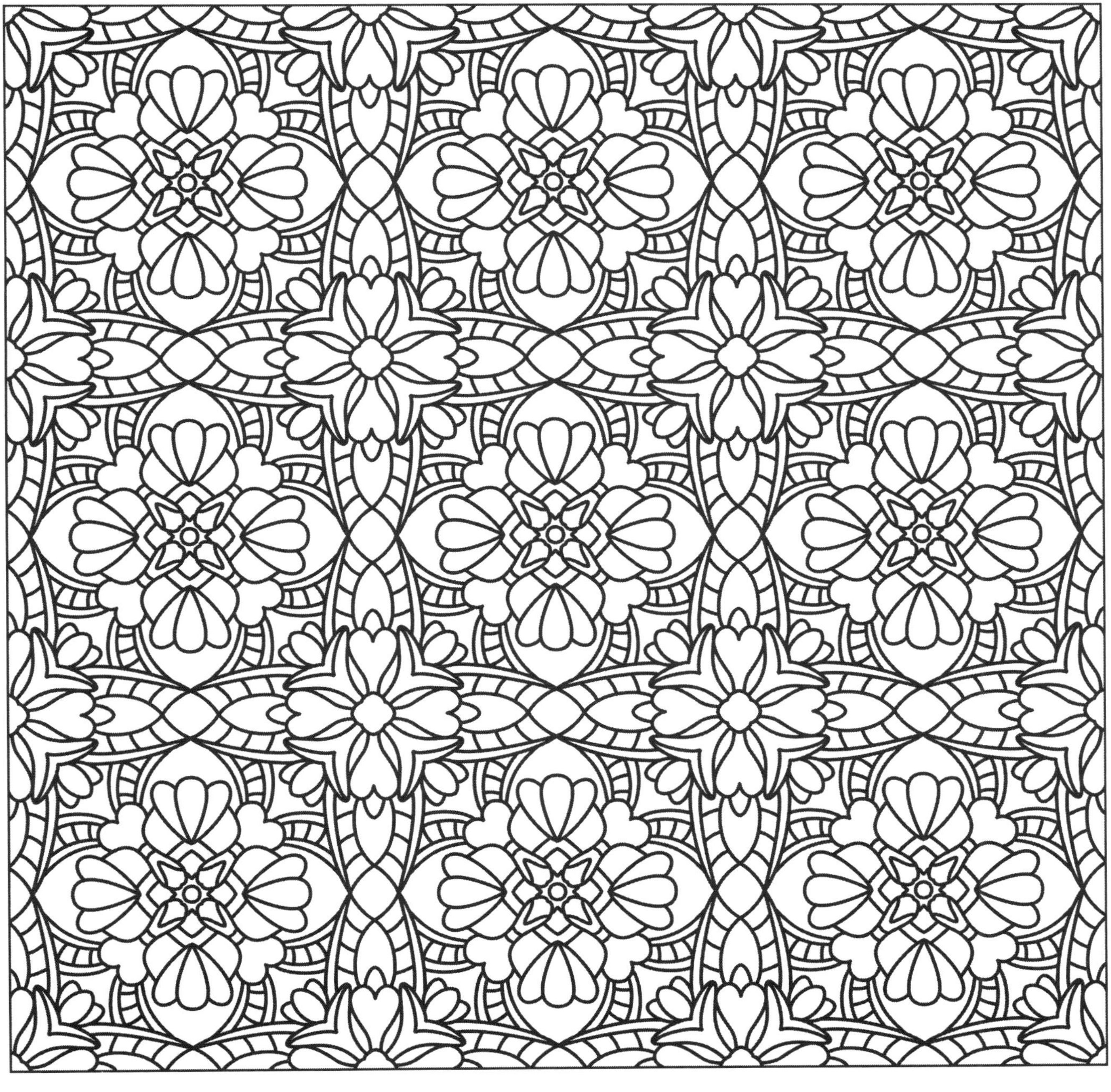

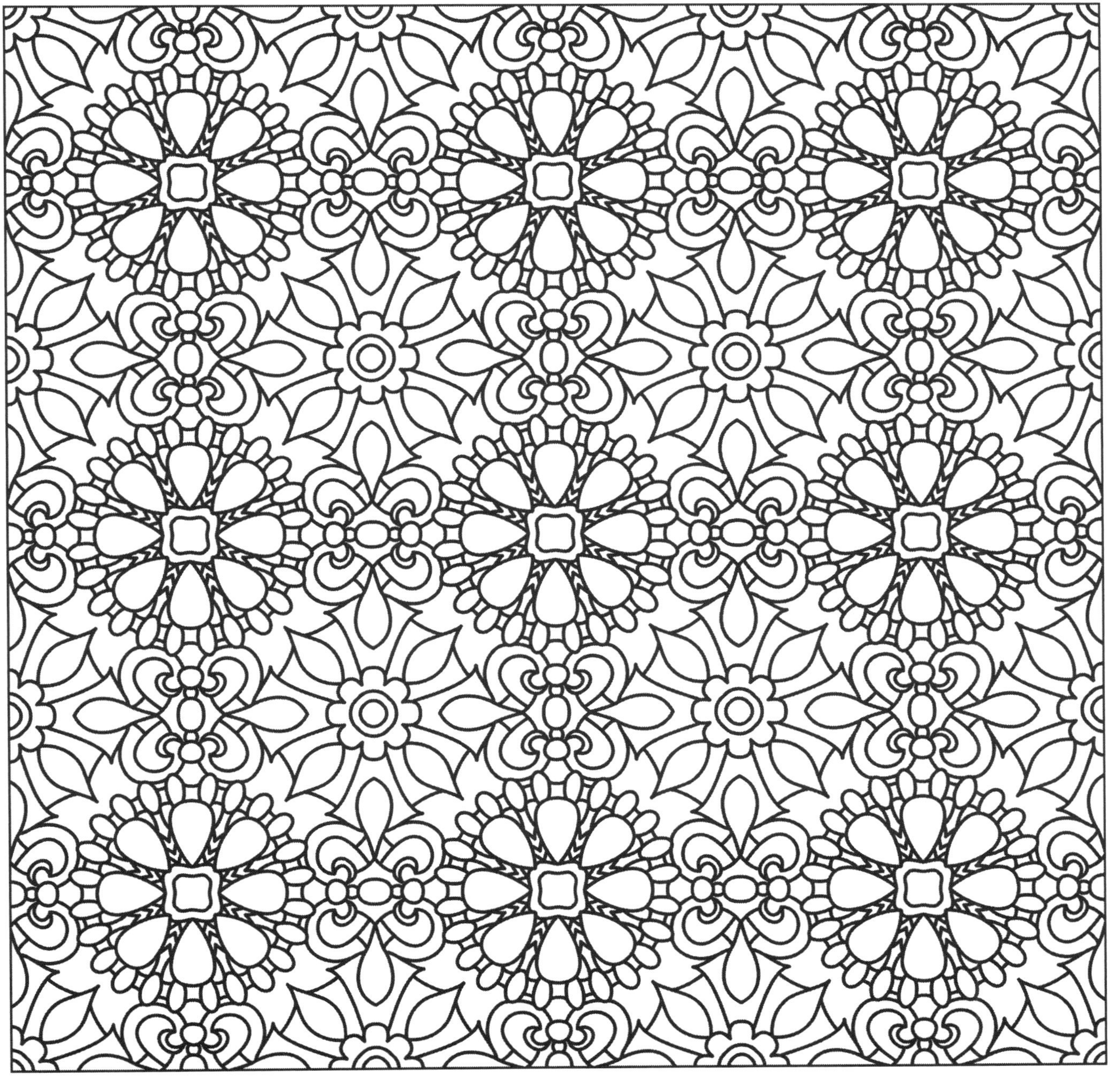

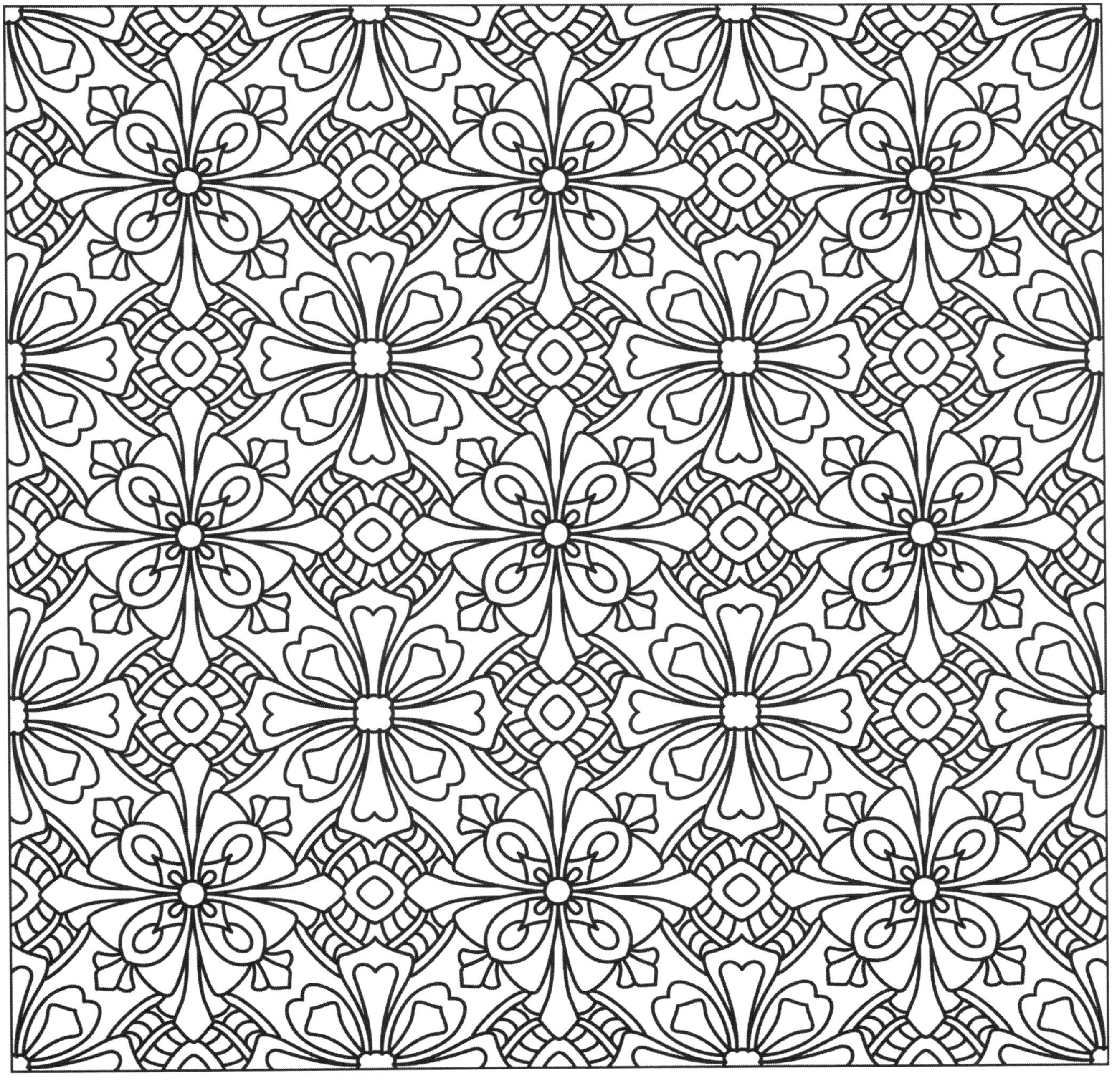

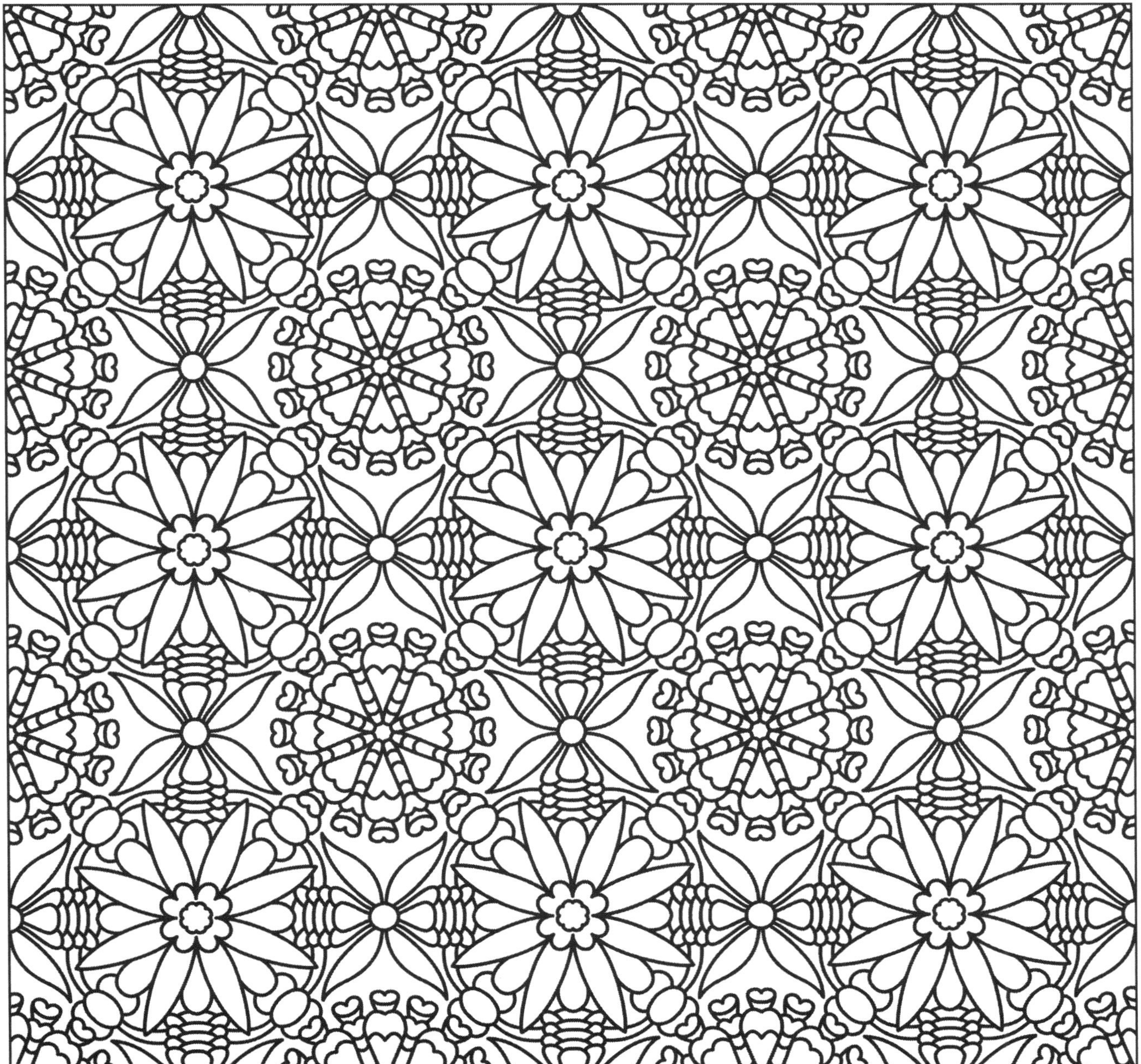

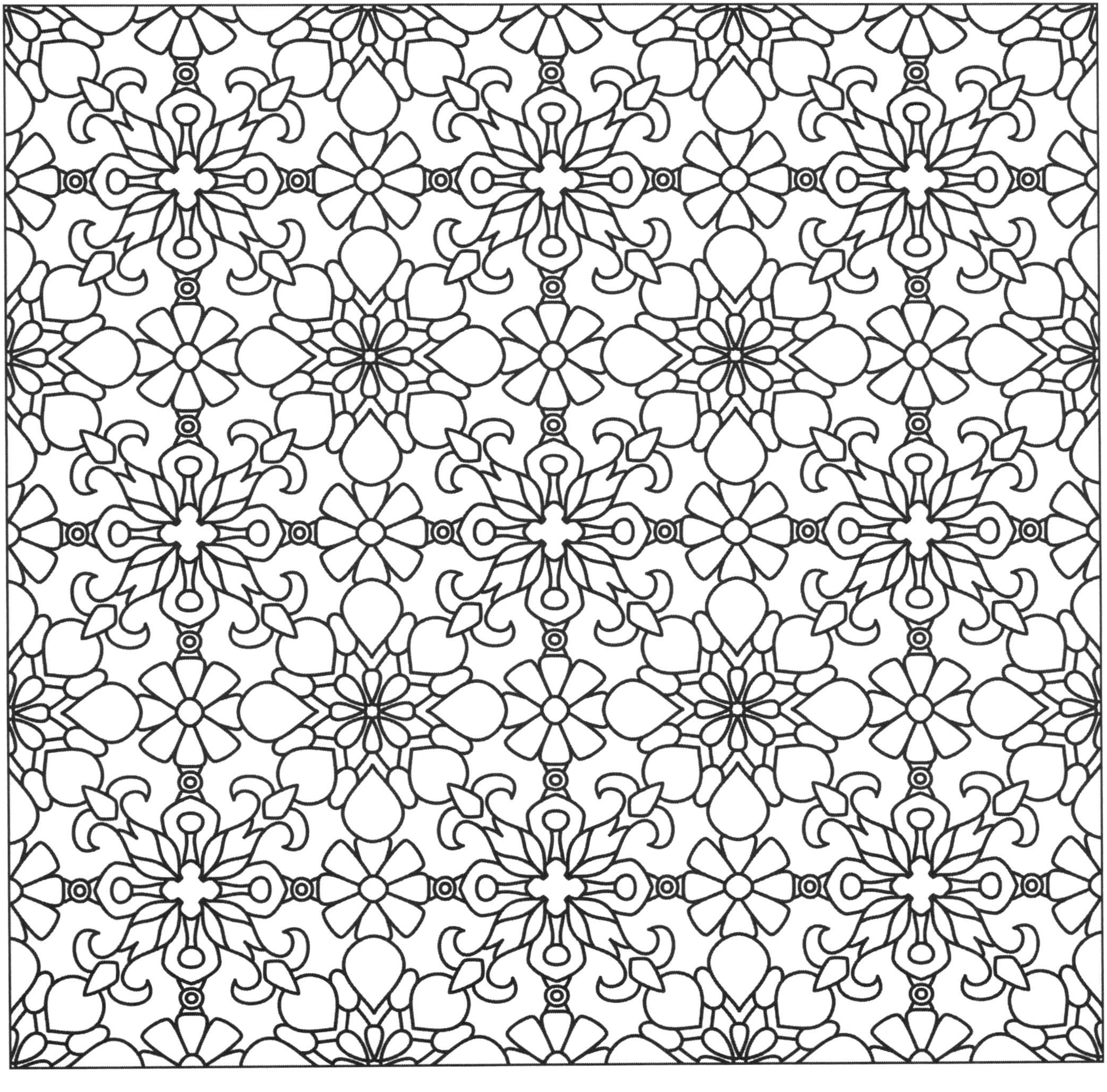

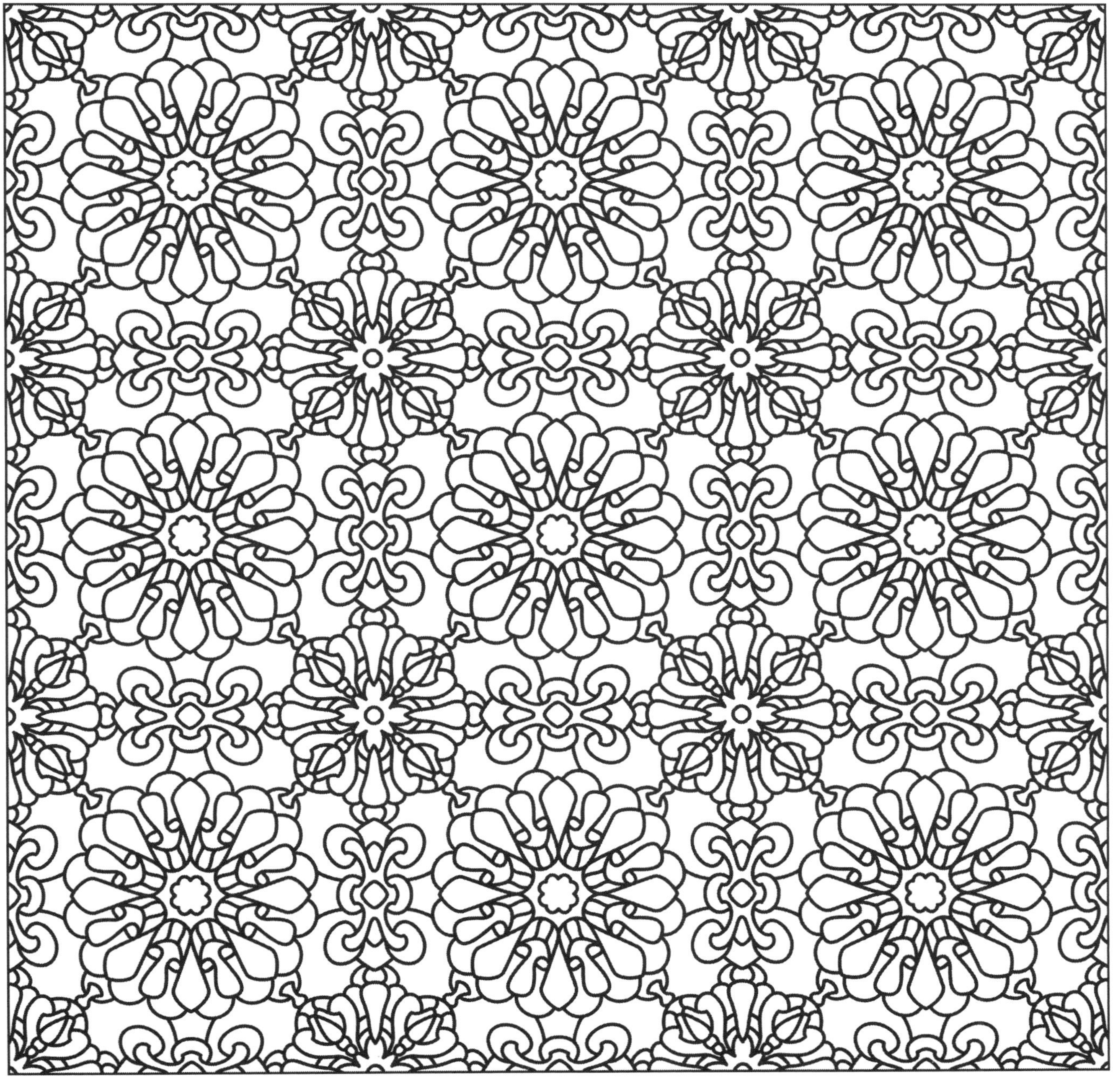

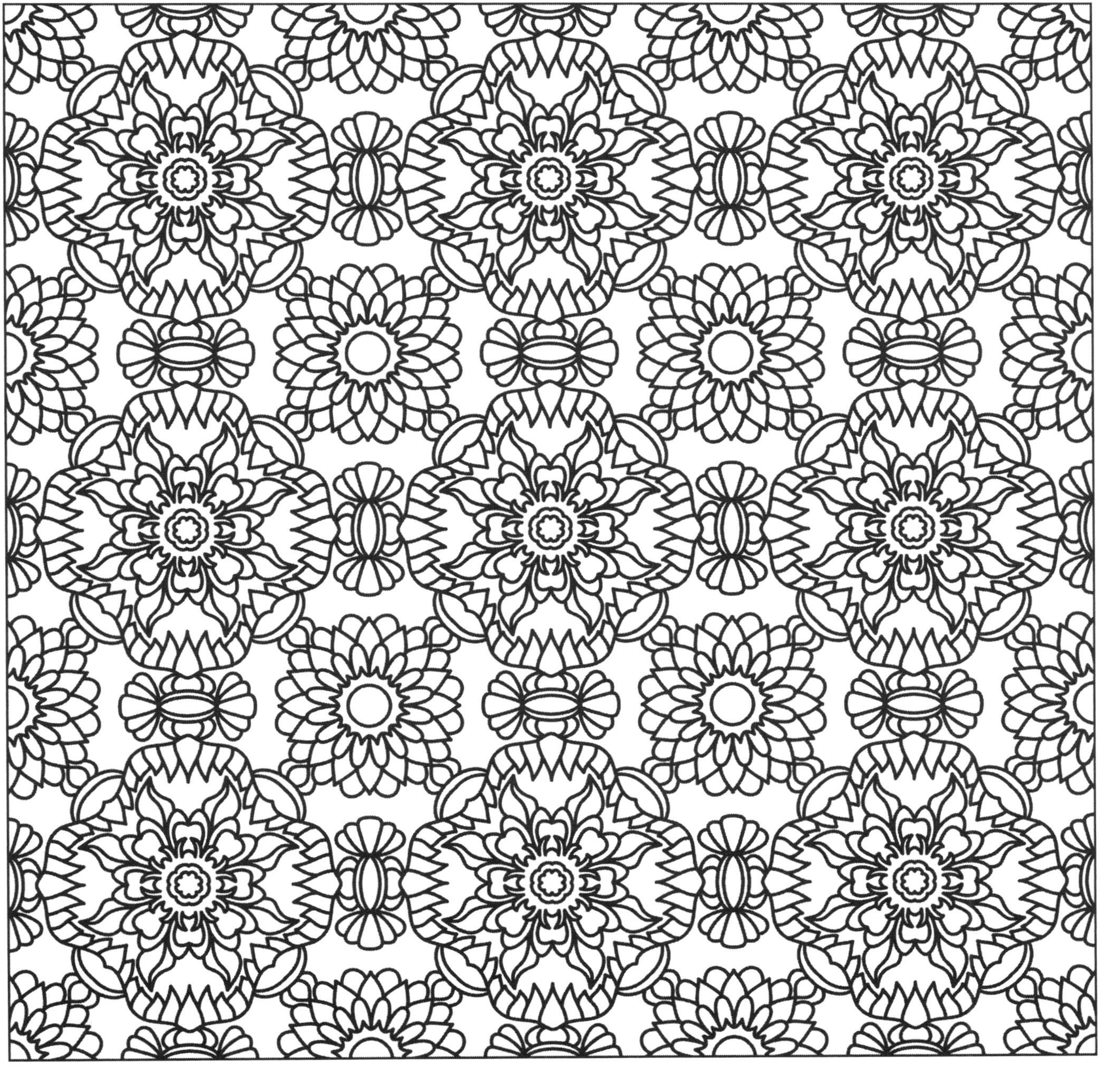

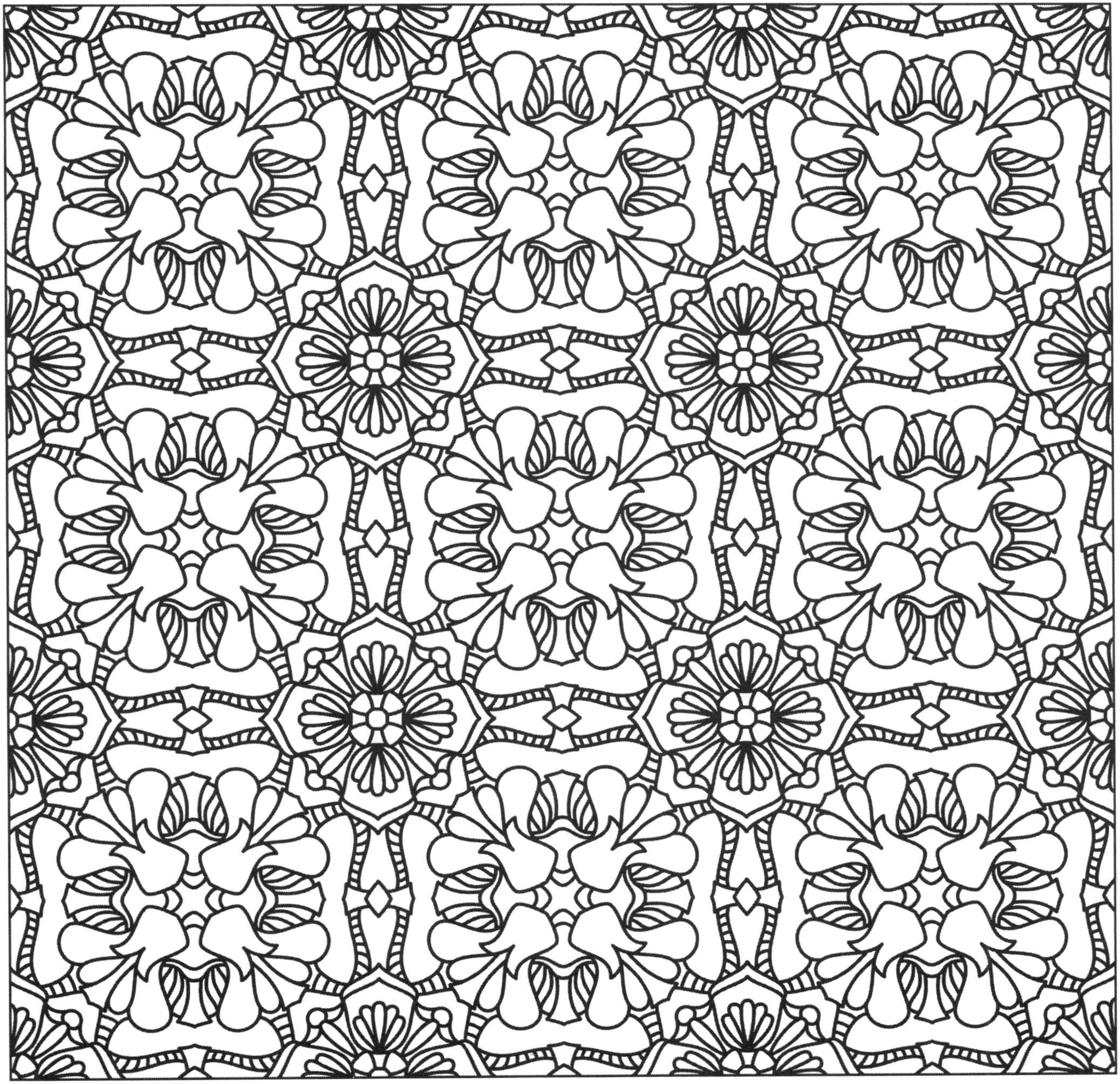

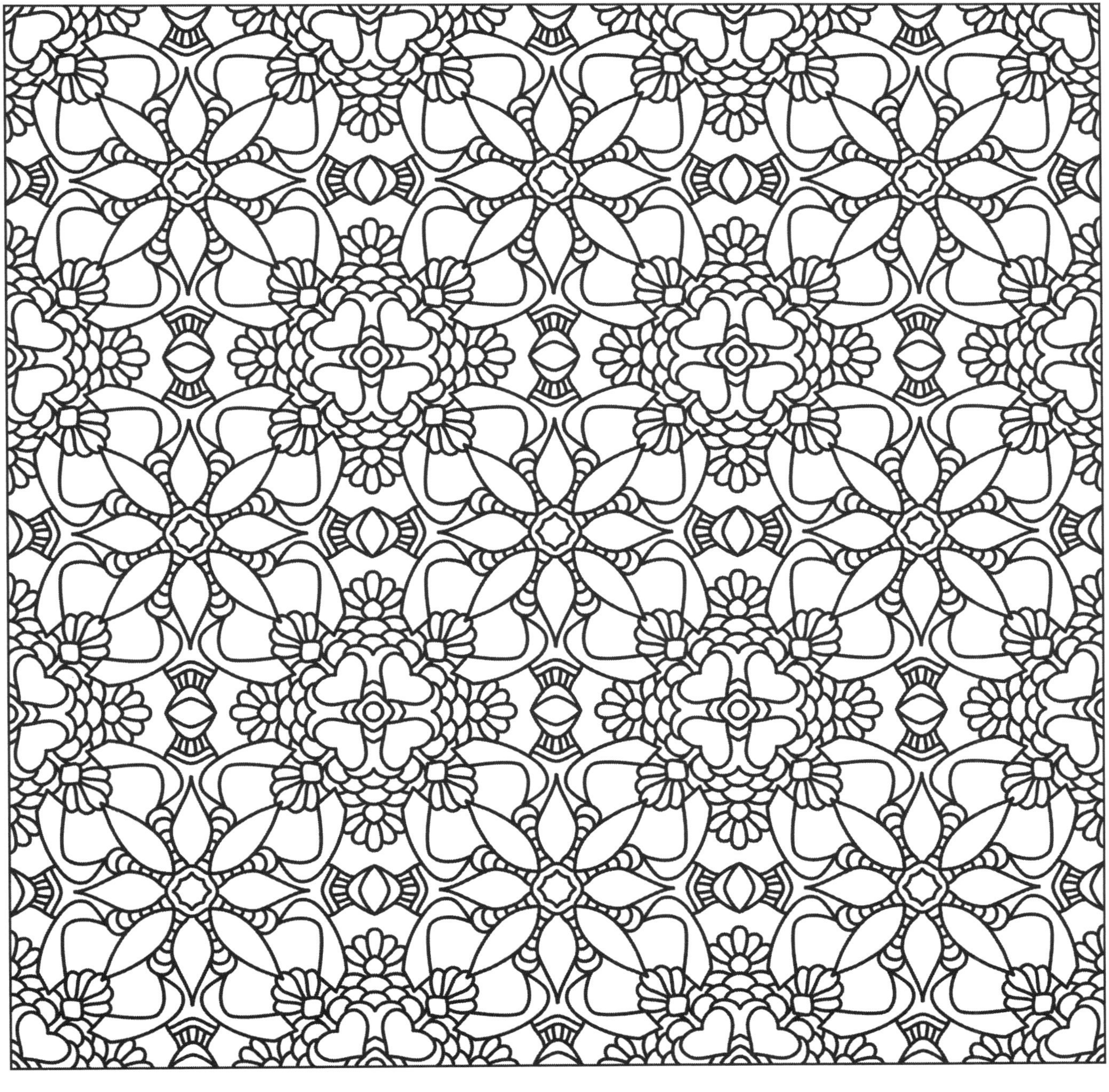

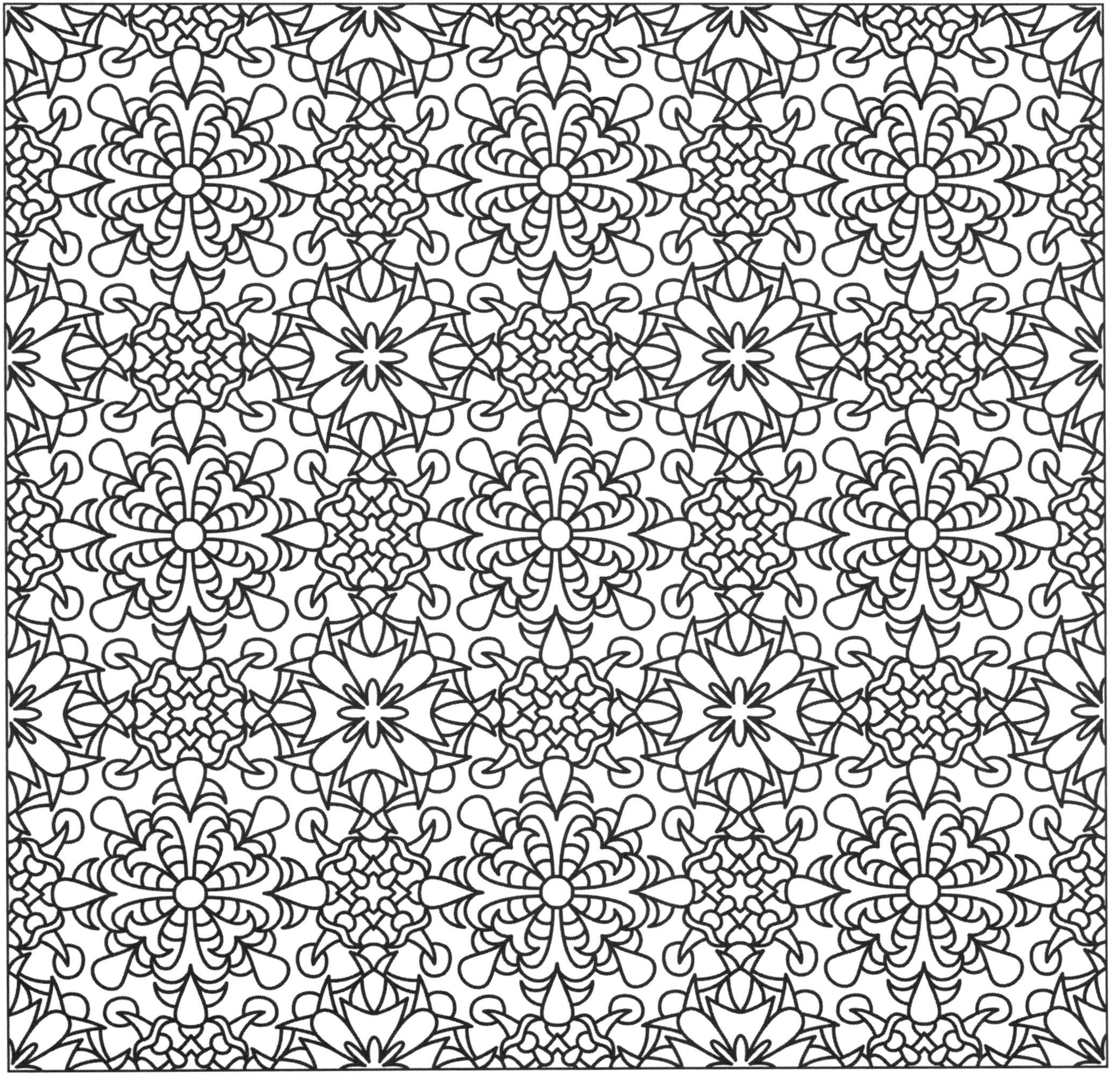

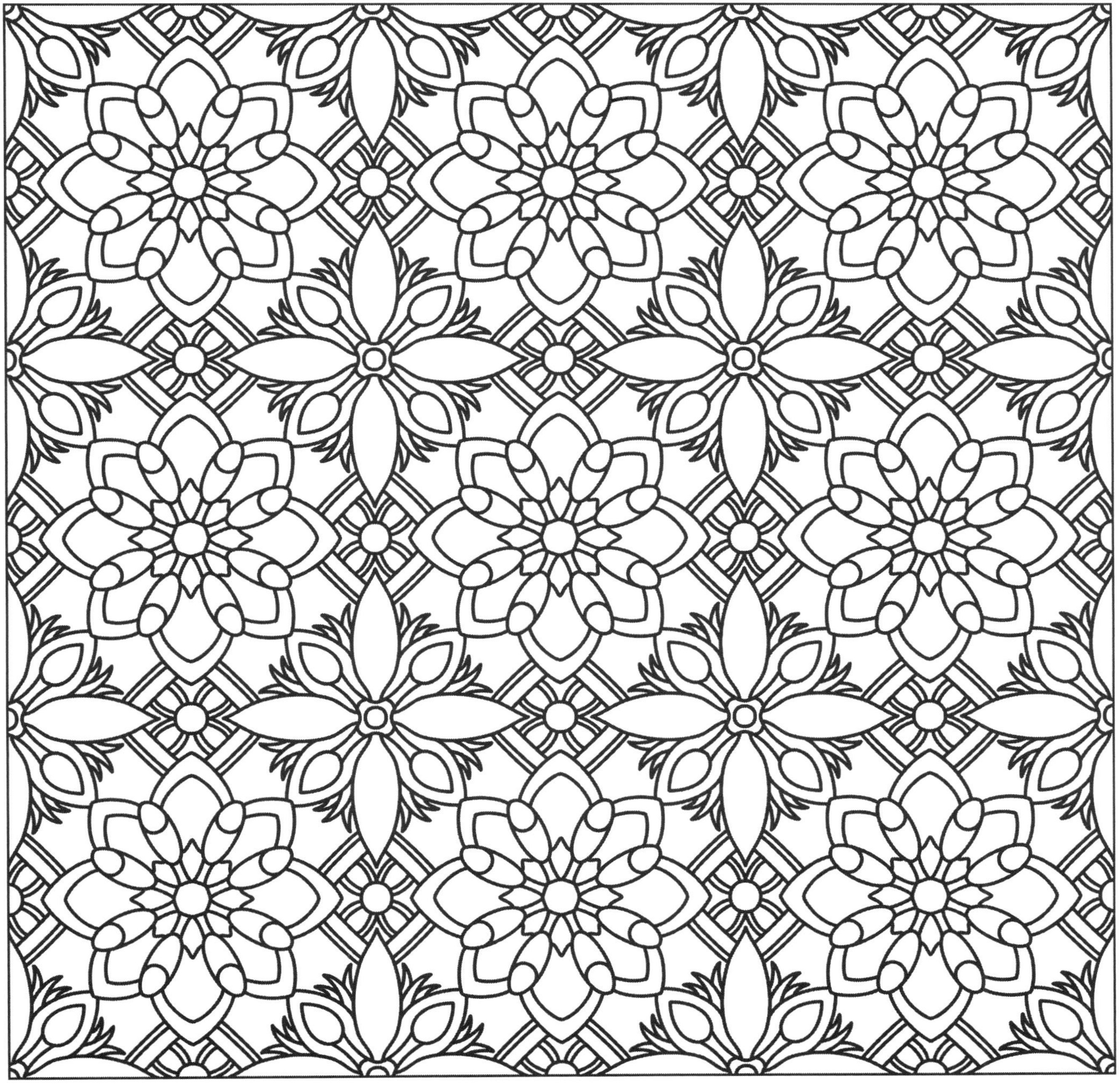

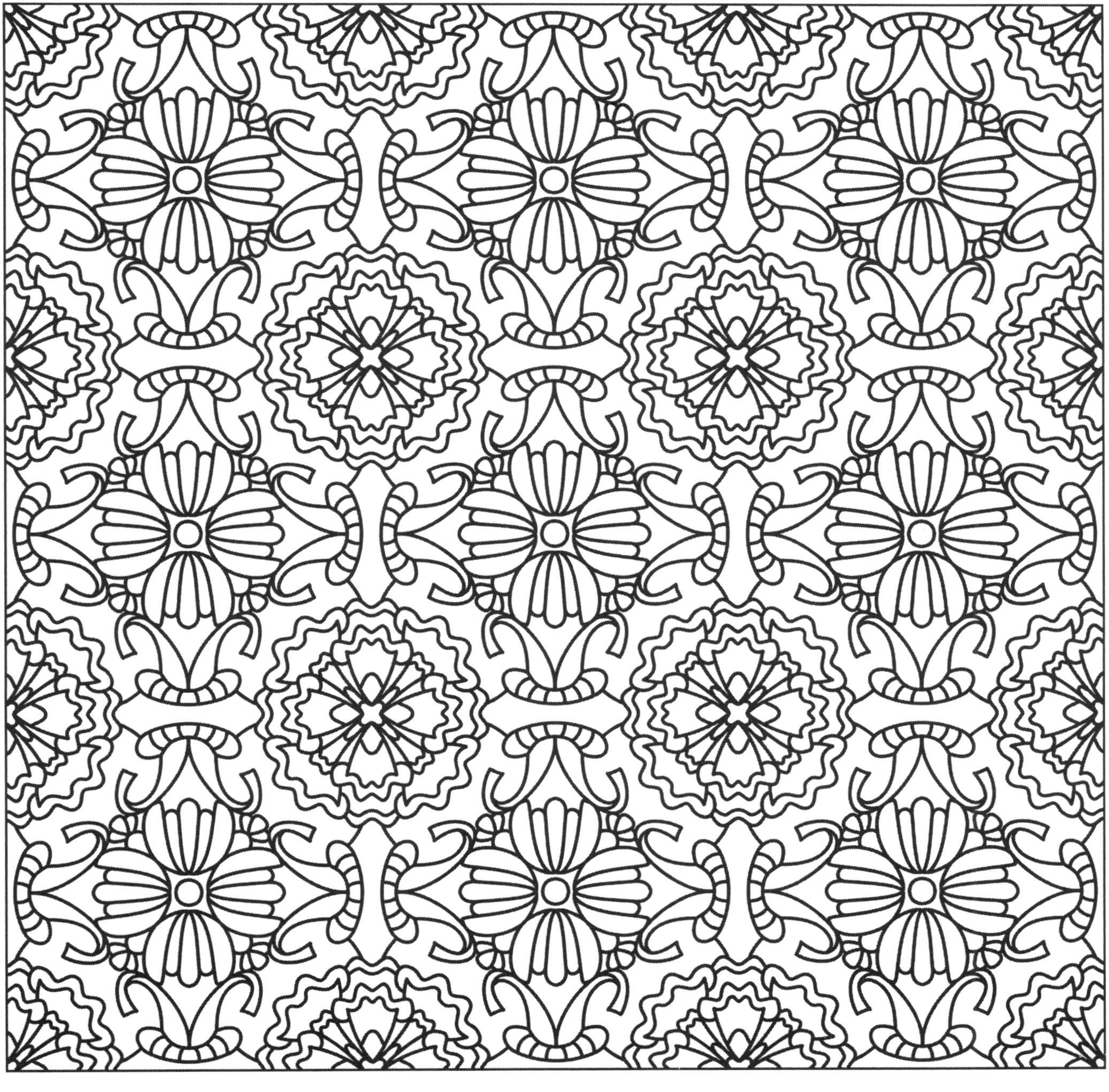

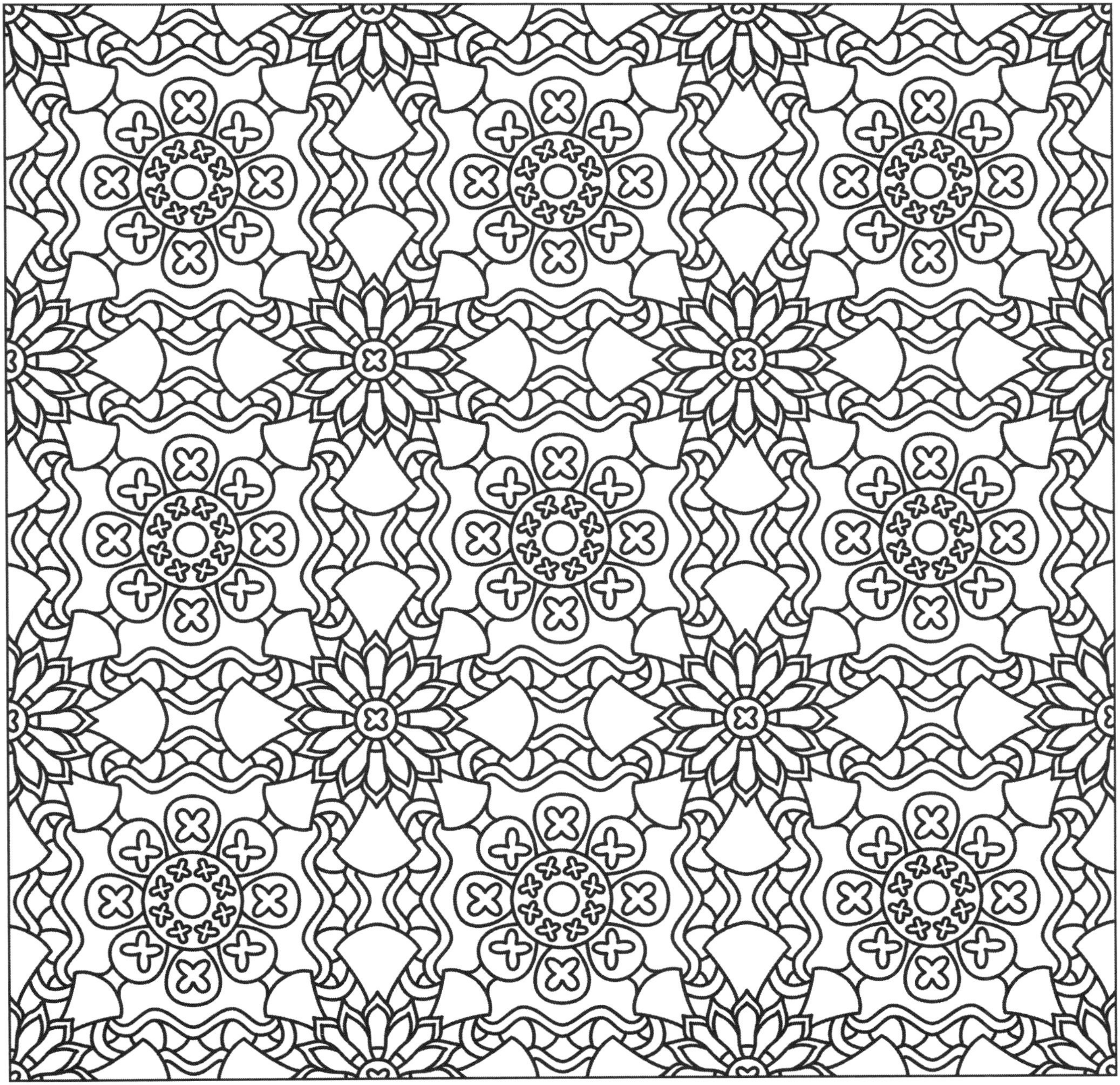

www.AngieGrace.com

Visit Angie's website for special web exclusives.

13037697R00060

Made in the USA
San Bernardino, CA
06 July 2014